PARAGRAPHS

Introduction (Elements of Paragraphing)

The Paragraph of Definition and Description

The Paragraph of Illustration and Example

The Paragraph of Comparison, Contrast, Analogy

The Paragraph of Reasoning

The Paragraph of Space, Time, Narration

The Opening and Concluding Paragraph

COMPACT HANDBOOK OF COLLEGE COMPOSITION

SECOND EDITION

Maynard J. Brennan
Saint Vincent College

D. C. HEATH AND COMPANY
Lexington, Massachusetts   Toronto   London

PREFACE

The aim of this revised *Handbook* is modest. It does not set out to be an esoteric book on rhetoric, a scholarly work on semantics and grammar, or a comprehensive survey of what to do in order to write well. It is simply a book concerned with fundamentals; it identifies and defines basic grammatical terms; it provides many hints about what not to do and some hints about what to do. A familiarity with the contents will not guarantee that the student emerges a polished, imaginative, even correct, writer; but it may help him to become a better writer than he was before he read the book.

It comes as a mild, though not infrequent, shock to teachers of college English that after twelve years of schooling most freshmen cannot differentiate between a complete and incomplete sentence, a restrictive and nonrestrictive clause, a colon and a semicolon. Resignedly teachers face up to reality and either teach basic grammar in the classroom or make available a handbook that will demonstrate with definite simplicity what acceptable writing is all about. Such a handbook of "definite simplicity" is this.

In the first section, this *Handbook* outlines, diagrams, and explains those aspects of usage and grammar that the student is most likely to find nebulous and difficult. The second section is an anthology of paragraphs that should stimulate the student's thinking, while providing him with varied examples of worthwhile, if not always distinguished, writing.

To know how to write a respectable paragraph is not to say that one can write a book or essay, but at least it is a step in the right direction. This *Handbook* presumes that, if a student can develop one idea with clarity and force, in time he may be able to develop and tie together many ideas.

It is interesting to observe how an author of a handbook can change within a half dozen years. What was a directive or dogma in the first edition of this book is now more often than not a suggestion. It is encouraging to know that a teacher may be more liberal even though older. To illustrate:

"He don't know nothing" may be the despair of English teachers, but the sentence is much more effective than the pallid "He doesn't know anything." "He doesn't care" causes no frowns at faculty meetings and tea parties, but "It don't make him no never mind," while it violates many conventions of grammar, is infinitely more colorful.

Bugaboos over split infinitives and double superlatives are rapidly disappearing. A split infinitive is many times a good way to effectively convey one's meaning. "This was the most unkindest cut of all" is exactly what Shakespeare wanted to say: He did not wish to say "This was the unkindest cut" or "This was the most unkind cut."

A half knowledge of grammar is a dangerous thing, sometimes worse than complete ignorance. Certain people, taught to say "You and I will see *Rigoletto* tonight" will sink to such absurdities as: "Just between you and I, when are we going to see *Rigoletto?*"

Let us suppose a young man is telephoning his girl friend to ask for a date. He asks, "Is this Margaret?" She responds: "This is she." In such a case the young man should hang up immediately. Chances are that the relationship will never work out. It's downright pretentious to say "It is I" when the natural thing to say is "It's me." So also, to say "With whom are you going" is not only stuffy but less natural than "Whom are you going with" and far less natural than "Who are you going with."

In essence, while this *Handbook* tries to preserve its respect for tradition and convention, it does not want to be stuffy or rigid. The form of expression or kind of grammar we use depends a great deal on particular occasions. It is much like wearing clothes. One does not wear beach clothes to a black-tie cocktail party, nor does one wear formal clothes to a beach. There is a time for this kind of dress and a time for that. So, also, there is a time for formal English and a time for colloquial; there are times, too, when only slang or those "dreadful" Anglo Saxon words are appropriate. The knack is to recognize each kind of time and to clothe our thoughts accordingly.

CONTENTS

USAGE

Diction

PARAGRAPHS

Introduction

The Paragraph of Definition and Description

The Paragraph of Illustration and Example

The Paragraph of Comparison, Contrast, Analogy

The Paragraph of Reasoning

The Paragraph of Space, Time, Narration

The Opening and Concluding Paragraph

COMPACT HANDBOOK OF COLLEGE COMPOSITION

USAGE

GRAMMATICAL TERMS AND DEFINITIONS

Parts of Speech

1. **Noun**—from Latin *nomen* (name)—a name of something, such as:

a person	John, girl, man
an action or place	race, fight, street, city, corner
a thing	tree, flower, desk
an animal	lion, elephant, mouse
a quality	mercy, goodness, sincerity

A noun may be modified only by another noun or an adjective (or by a phrase or clause functioning as an adjective).

2. **Pronoun**—from Latin *pro-nomen* (for a name)—a word used in place of a noun. A pronoun can be modified by an adjective or by a phrase or clause acting as an adjective substitute.

A. Personal Pronoun

Personal pronouns change their inflectional forms according to their case (subjective or nominative, genitive or possessive, and objective), according to their gender (masculine, feminine, or neuter), according to the person indicated (first person, second person, or third person), and according to their number (singular or plural).

		1st person	*2nd person*	
Singular:	subj.	I	you	
	gen.	my, mine	your, yours	
	obj.	me	you	
Plural:	subj.	we		
	gen.	our, ours	(same as singular)	
	obj.	us		

		3rd person		
		masc.	*fem.*	*neut.*
Singular:	subj.	he	she	it
	gen.	his	her, hers	its
	obj.	him	her	it

3

Plural:	subj.	they	(plural shows
	gen.	their, theirs	no difference
	obj.	them	in gender)

B. Demonstrative Pronoun

Singular:	this	that
Plural:	these	those

C. Relative Pronoun

In reference to persons:

subj.	who
gen.	whose
obj.	whom

(These pronouns show no difference between singular and plural.)

In reference to animals, inanimate objects, and abstractions:

subj.	which
gen.	whose, of which, of what
obj.	which, what

In reference to persons, animals, inanimate objects, and abstractions:

that (no inflections)

Variations of relative pronouns:

whoever   whatever   whomever   whichever   whosoever
whatsoever,   etc.

D. Interrogative Pronoun

who   which   what

(forms for *who* and *which* are the same as for the relative pronoun)

E. Indefinite Pronoun

anyone, any, some, someone, no one, nobody, everyone, everybody, each one, each, all, none

F. Intensive and Reflexive Pronoun

  myself, yourself, himself, herself, itself
  ourselves, yourselves, themselves

G. Reciprocal Pronoun

  each other, one another

3. **Adjective**—from Latin *ad-jacere* (to add to)—a word that modifies, describes, qualifies, limits the concept given by a noun. Adjectives may be modified by adverbs (or by a clause or phrase functioning as an adverb substitute).

   two miles, *evil* intentions, *beautiful* sky, *few* friends, *the* plan, *a* book, *an* apple (note: *the, a, an* are also referred to as articles)

4. **Verb**—from Latin *verbum* (a word)—a word that makes an assertion, or an action performed or suffered by the subject. Verbs are modified only by adverbs (or by clauses and phrases with that function).

   A. *Transitive* Verb

     One that may use an object to complete its meaning (i.e., that may transmit the verb's action to an object).

     e.g., He *made* a doorway (for the house).

   B. *Intransitive* Verb

     One that does not use an object to complete its meaning (i.e., cannot transmit action to any object).

     e.g., He *sits* (under the pavilion roof at noon) and *lies* (in the sun at three).

   C. *Linking* Verb

     One that connects or links the subject of the sentence with a classification or modification of the subject. The linking verb thus connects the subject with a predicate noun (or a phrase or clause acting as a noun substitute) or with an adjective (or adjective substitute).

e.g., Fred *is* a sailor.
He *looks* handsome.
The time *is* now.
It *tastes* good.

D. *Active* Verb

One that indicates an action which the subject of the sentence performs directly.

e.g., Jackson *hit* his opponent (on the jaw).
John *moved* the book (to the table).

E. *Passive* Verb

One that indicates an action suffered or received by the subject of the sentence; the performer of the action is indicated (if at all) by a prepositional phrase.

e.g., The opponent *was hit* (by Jackson).
The book *was moved* (by John).

F. *Verbals*—forms of the verb

Verbals function in sentences as nouns, adjectives, or adverbs, rather than as main verbs. Like main verbs, however, verbals can be modified by adverbs or adverbial clauses and phrases, and they can be transitive, intransitive, active, or passive.

F(1). *Participle*—a verbal

A form of a verb used as an adjective to modify a noun or pronoun.

e.g.,The *singing* bird—the *sighing* lover—the *broken* leg—the slowly *curving* road—a man *being pushed* is uncomfortable

F(2). *Infinitive*—a verbal

A form of the verb preceded usually by *to*—the infinitive phrase may function as a noun, an adjective, or an adverb.

as a noun:

To sing is *to love.*
To be pushed is uncomfortable.

He prefers *to sing* in cabarets.
To report misdemeanors is good policy.

as an adjective:

There were many pictures *to see*, and more *to be seen*.
The time *to take* action is now.

as an adverb:

Jack was reluctant *to go*: he is unhappy *to be gone*. (modify adjectives *reluctant* and *unhappy*)
She is going *to see* the museum. (modifies verb *is going*)

F(3). *Gerund*—a verbal

A form of the verb ending in *ing* and used as a noun.

e.g., *Swimming* is good exercise.
Marion likes spirited *singing*.
His *going* so soon left me amazed.

5. **Adverb**—from Latin *ad-verbum* (something added to a verb or word)—a word that modifies a verb, adjective, or another adverb.

a verb:

He plays his cards *calmly*.
He *evidently* lost his temper.

an adjective:

Jane is *extremely* gracious.
Joan is *somewhat* sad.

another adverb:

He talks *very* graciously.
She plays the piano *rather* well.

6. **Preposition**—from Latin *pre-ponere* (to place before)—a word or group of words used before a noun or pronoun (or before a noun clause) to make a prepositional phrase that modifies another word. The noun or pronoun in the phrase is called an *object* of the preposition.

e.g., He arrived *on* foot, but he was *in* time.
There is no honor *among* thieves.
Read the chapter *before* nine and not *after*.

7. Conjunction—from Latin *con-jungere* (to join with)—a word used to join or connect other words, or phrases, or clauses.

> words:
>
> Mother *and* Father . . .
> God *or* country . . .
> in *or* out . . .
> push *and* pull . . .
>
> phrases:
>
> She is *either* working in the dairy *or* sunning herself.
> Under ordinary circumstances *and* barring unforeseen accidents, you will succeed.
>
> clauses:
>
> *Because* he was malicious . . . he was disliked.
> *Although* he came late for lunch . . . he ate greedily.
> *In case* you hadn't heard . . . we have no bananas.
> Yours is an appealing argument, *but* unfortunately it is not realistic.
> It was late *when* we arrived.

8. Interjection—from Latin *inter-jacere* (to throw between)—a word that expresses emotion and sometimes hesitation, but is not necessary to the sentence's grammatical meaning.

> e.g., *Well*, you have finally arrived.
> *Oh*, I don't know about that.
> *Ah*, I see that you finally agreed to my terms.
> The cost will be—*oh*—two dollars.

The Sentence

1. Complete Sentence—A complete sentence makes an assertion (a statement, question, or command)—in other words it does not leave the hearer or reader hanging in the air wondering what the speaker or writer is saying. Grammatically, it must always be complete with at least two elements: subject and predicate. Thus it must say something (predicate) about something (subject). Completeness or lack of completeness is not a question of length. For instance, "Snow melts" is a complete sentence, but "Because he did not heed the lecturer's advice and because he was forgetful many times in important matters" is an incomplete sentence despite the fact that it is considerably longer than "Snow melts."

A. Complete sentence with intransitive verb (refer to page 5 for the definition of intransitive verb):

Babies (subject) | cry (predicate)

B. Complete sentence with transitive verb, transmitting the verb's action to an object (refer to page 5 for the definition of transitive verb):

John (subject) | throws (predicate) | stones (object)

C. Complete sentence with verb that links the subject (noun or noun substitute) with a predicate noun:

Kennedy (subject) | was (predicate) \ President (pred. noun)

D. Complete sentence with verb that links the subject (noun or noun substitute) with a modifying predicate adjective:

Skies (subject) | are (predicate) \ blue (pred. adj.)

2. **Incomplete Sentence or Fragment**—An incomplete sentence or fragment is one that does not make an assertion or, in other words, leaves one with the impression that the speaker or writer has not thought out what he wishes to say. Every sentence must contain a subject and verb with an independent basic structure. (Occasionally in conversational dialogue, subject or predicate may be implicit: e.g., "Back already?" In this case, "Are you" is clearly implied. Also, the imperative verb does not have an explicit subject: e.g., "Fight!") In written or spoken exposition a missing subject or predicate leaves the sentence incomplete.

A. Fragment: Because the government collapsed.

This has a subject (government) and a predicate (collapsed), but *because* makes the group of words subordinate, or dependent, upon a further assertion that is missing.

B. Fragment: The house standing on the corner and looking like a mid-Victorian classic.

This has a subject, but no finite verb; thus an object is named, and then qualified or modified by verbals acting as adjectives, but no assertion is made.

Revised: The house *stood* on the corner and *looked* like . . .

C. Fragment: Because of constant laziness and general indifference.

This is nothing more than a subordinate phrase with neither subject nor predicate which the phrase might modify.

Revised: He failed because of laziness and general indifference.

Note: Although even fine writers will use fragments, they use them for a definite literary purpose, knowing full well what fragments and complete sentences are. A word of caution, then: do not use a fragment without having a definite purpose in mind and without recognizing that it *is* a fragment.

3. **Compound Sentence**—A compound sentence is one that has at least two independent clauses (see below, "the clause"), each capable of being recognized and treated as a simple sentence. The independent clauses are usually joined by a semicolon or by a comma and a conjunction. A compound sentence makes one type of coordinate (or parallel) sentence structure.*

A. The meetings were entertaining, but the results (were) negligible.

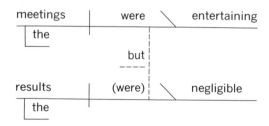

---

*Coordinate means of equal degree or importance; in other words, one part or item cannot be subordinate to another. E.g., the door of a room and the room itself are not coordinate; an independent clause and a dependent one are not coordinate.

B. The stars were bright, the music soft, all was perfect.

```
stars    |   were    \   bright
   | the |
              (and)
music    |  (was)    \   soft
   | the |
              (and)
all      |   was     \   perfect
```

C. Harvard had a successful season, but Yale did not.

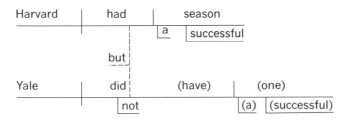

Note: Do not confuse a compound sentence with a simple sentence that uses a compound (multiple) subject or a compound (multiple) predicate or both.

Thus a) Both Astaire and Hope sang and danced. (compound subject and predicate)

   b) The college revised its policy and became coeducational. (compound predicate)

   c) All-American football players and Miss Americas sometimes wed. (compound subject)

a)

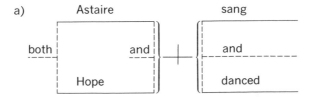

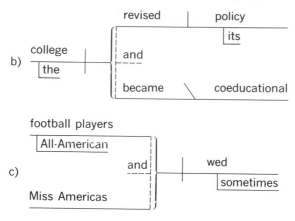

b)

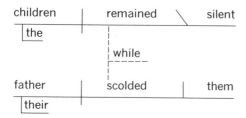

c)

Note: Avoid overuse of coordinate structure in long compound sentences.

Weak: There was a long delay, and he waited for the moonlight, and then he led the crew into a deep cavern, and there the fight began.

Better: There was a long delay while he waited for the moonlight; then he led the crew into a deep cavern where the fight began.

4. Complex Sentence—A complex sentence is one that contains a main independent clause (often capable of being treated as a complete sentence) and one or more dependent clauses (see below, "the clause"), which form a dependent part of some element in the main clause. Or a complex sentence is one with a subordinate clause.

A. Complex sentence with a subordinate *adverbial* clause (see below "the clause").

e.g., The children remained silent while their father scolded them.

children | remained \ silent
the |
| while
father | scolded | them
their |

B. Complex sentence with dependent *adjectival* clause.

e.g., Hubert Humphrey, who is a Democrat, lost the presidential race.

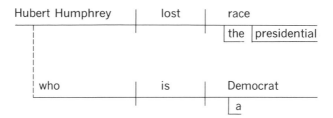

C. Complex sentence with dependent *noun* clause.

e.g., She announced that she would run for office.

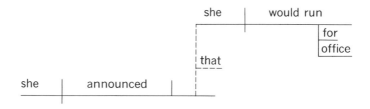

EXERCISE I

Identify each sentence as simple, compound, or complex, and indicate the subject and predicate of each independent clause. (The subject should be underlined once and the predicate twice.)

1. Isabelle's smile vanished when she saw her image in the mirror.

2. She wanted to get out of her bed and begin to work like a normal person again.

3. On the way to the theater she met a classmate whom she had not seen in years.

4. Jack had been too stupid to realize that business is never consistently good, that there had to be recessions.

5. Val went and sat apart, his sadness deepening.

6. Thursday grandmother sat with her maid in the sunshine till the last possible moment, went to lie down at five, and slept until seven.

7. Martha, walking back and forth, brushing her hair, resented the presence of her mother-in-law and took no pains to hide her impatience.

8. It was hard to predict what the possibilities of success were.

9. When they dined in the evening, they were most careful not to attract attention.

10. When will you return and finish the project?

11. For ten years she traveled to Europe each summer, but suddenly travel became boring to her.

12. Death, even if it came unexpectedly, could not defeat her scheme.

13. There lay in front of her, on the oak table, an enormous bunch of flowers, just freshly cut.

14. He looked as though he were the victim of a cruel jest.

15. He turned out the lights and opened the front door, waiting for her to enter.

The Clause

A clause contains both subject and predicate in a unit of words that combines with other such units, thus forming a compound, complex, or compound-complex sentence. A compound sentence combines on an equal (coordinate) basis at least two *independent clauses,* each of which may be regarded as a complete sentence. In a complex sentence, clauses are combined in an independent-dependent relationship—at least one *dependent* (subordinate) *clause* modifying or forming a part of an element in the *main clause.* Dependent clauses have three kinds of subordinate relationship to the main clause.

1. Adverbial Clause—It can show comparison, condition, manner, place, purpose, result, time, concession, provision, or cause. It is introduced by such adverbial conjunctions as: *when, while, where, as, since, because, after, before, although, if, so, in order that, than,* and *where.* An adverbial clause usually modifies a verb. (Occasionally it may also modify an adjective, a prepositional phrase, or a verbal.)

clause—adjectival

A. Although the sun was shining, he was irritable.

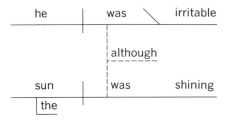

B. Jack is stronger than Jim.

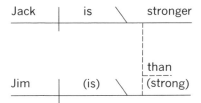

C. Go out into the deep water if you wish to catch many fish.

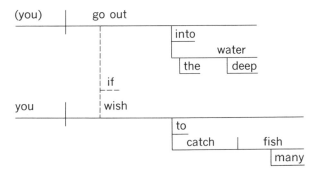

2. **Adjectival Clause**—It is a relative clause that depends upon a noun or pronoun. It is usually introduced by a relative pronoun such as: *who, that, which, what, whom, whoever, whomever.*

A. The car I bought was a Ford.

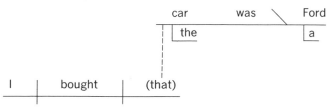

B. You should choose Gloria, who is tastefully dressed.

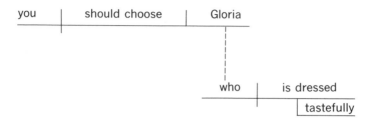

C. I know the person who is protesting.

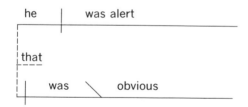

3. **Noun Clause**—It is one whose function is the same as that of a noun in the sentence. It is usually introduced by *that, what, where.*

A. Noun clause as a subject of a sentence: That he was alert was obvious.

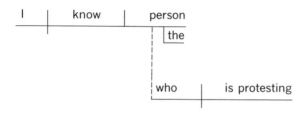

B. Noun clause as object of a sentence: He knew that the search was futile.

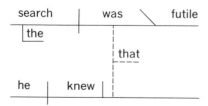

C. Noun clause as object of a preposition: Your success will depend upon how well you do your assignments.

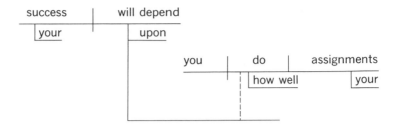

EXERCISE II

Underline the dependent clauses in the following sentences, and indicate whether they are adverbial, adjectival, or noun clauses.

1. Research into success has often hinted that some people are more equal than others.

2. Though one may feel that it is too bad John Dos Passos did not visit the island and write his last book, *Easter Island: Island of Enigmas,* as a younger man, one's glad to have it on these terms.

3. While no appeal had been made from the original desegregation order, every effort was made to stall the court order to implement it.

4. The lyrics from *Jesus Christ Superstar* are contemporary and often idiomatic; but, as an English critic has pointed out, it is just as legitimate as Handel's version of *The Messiah,* which "similarly clothed the Christian story in the language, verbal and melodic, of its day."

5. He has a slender hold on reality. The horrors, real and imaginary, that Jack evokes are clearly beyond his ability to grasp.

6. Only 14 when he got his first electric guitar, Pete managed to put in 17 years on the instrument that was to make him famous.

7. Obviously if psychiatry merely helps the patient adjust to a sick society so that he can function in it, it only moves him from one kind of sickness to another.

8. "If ever there has been a looser construction of the Constitution in this

court's history," said Justice Hugo Black in a blistering ad lib accom-
panying his written dissent, "I fail to think what it is."

9. His fellow actors often express admiration of George C. Scott because
   he has the courage to risk professional failures.

10. It is important to note that the modest levels of Chinese support for
    revolutionary struggles abroad cannot be credited to constraints im-
    posed by U.S. policy.

PUNCTUATION

Introduction

Many students regard punctuation as arbitrary and superfluous. Worst of all, its study is boring. To a certain extent, their reaction is understandable. But punctuation is not a ridiculous whim foisted on us by pedants and hapless teachers who have nothing better to do. True, the system of punctuation we have inherited is conventional and sometimes questionable. Often correct, scrupulous usage is overemphasized to the detriment of more important elements of writing, such as ideas, diction, organization, imagination, and imagery.

On the other hand, let us not underrate the importance of correct formal punctuation, for incorrect usage can lead to misreading and misinterpretation. Then, too, most customs in punctuating are based on logic and common sense. Good writers do not rest their literary laurels on proper punctuation alone: they must have many other talents going for them. But whatever these talents may be, writers are conscious of the advantage of right usage. Good writers, as a rule, observe proper punctuation. The converse is not always true: proper punctuation by itself does not prove that any particular writer is a great or even a good one.

This section of the *Handbook*, therefore, is intended to help the writer. It makes no pretensions at solving all his problems.

Main Uses of the Comma

PRINCIPLE ONE

Independent clauses joined by a conjunction (*and, but, for, nor, so, yet*) are separated by a comma.

Examples:

> He has a fine sense of proportion, *but* for some unknown reason he has not succeeded at home or office.
>
> Students can plan their study carefully throughout the semester, *or* they can foolishly depend on last-minute cramming.

I would not place faith in the word of a thief, *nor* would I advise you to do so.

The supermarket is already closed, *yet* several clerks are still working at the meat counter.

It had rained constantly throughout the day, *so* they had little hope of playing the scheduled game.

Note: As a general rule, avoid the use of *so* in this sense. By subordinating one clause you can usually end with a better sentence:

> e.g., Because it had rained constantly throughout the day, they had little hope of playing the scheduled game.

A correct use of *so*:

> Beatrice retired from the office so that I could succeed her. Not: "so I could succeed her."

Note: A comma before the conjunction *for* distinguishes it from the preposition *for*, thus helping to obviate a misreading. Note the difference in these two sentences:

> a) We should not condemn the coach, *for* his efforts were sincere and time-consuming.
> b) We should not condemn the coach *for* his efforts.

PRINCIPLE TWO

In a coordinate series use commas to separate

> 1. three or more words
> 2. three or more phrases
> 3. three or more clauses

Example 1A: three or more words.

He stopped to admire $\begin{cases} \text{the huge,} \\ \text{gray,} \\ \text{foreboding} \end{cases}$ castle.

Explanation: If the meaning allows you to place *and* between the adjectives that modify a noun then they are coordinate and therefore demand commas. Thus the sentence above could read, "He stopped to admire the huge and gray and foreboding castle."

> Thus: She was wearing a light brown suit.
> (The color of the suit was light brown.)
>
> She was wearing a light, brown suit.
> (The suit was light in weight and brown in color.)

Example 1B: three or more words.

> The migrating "Oakie" families participated in each other's joys, griefs, deaths, and poverty.

Explanation: Although it is not necessary to insert a comma before the last items of a series when they are joined by *and,* many grammarians recommend that it be inserted. (This is the preference of the MLA *Style Sheet,* p. 9, N. 14B. The *Style Sheet* is a useful standard reference pamphlet published by the Modern Language Association.)

This comma prevents a misreading of such compound items as *bacon and eggs, milk and honey, cheese and crackers,* and the like.

> Thus: His breakfast consisted of fruit juice, coffee, and bacon and eggs. The combination is "bacon and eggs," not "coffee and bacon and eggs." (Do not make a fuss over this distinction: it is only a minor point more often honored in the breach than the observance.)

Example 2: three or more phrases.

A gentleman must have
$$\begin{cases} \text{patience in dealing with the faults of others,} \\ \text{kindness for the underprivileged,} \\ \text{consideration for the feelings of others.} \end{cases}$$

Example 3: three or more clauses.

We should admire a man
$$\begin{cases} \text{who has intelligence enough to make correct decisions,} \\ \text{who has courage enough to make bold decisions,} \\ \text{who has wit enough to make rapid decisions.} \end{cases}$$

PRINCIPLE THREE

Introductory adverbial clauses are set off by commas.

Examples:

> *Although it was nearly noon* (intro. adv. clause)**,** the sky was overcast and dark (main clause).
>
> *After the lawyer had defended the dentist's action,* most of the women jurists applauded.
>
> *When he was lonely and badly in need of consolation,* he often sought the hospitality of the aborigines.
>
> *Because his pride was unbending,* he was incapable of making the necessary adjustment to a hostile society.
>
> *As soon as one reaches the top of Mount Olivet,* he is filled with memories of its historical importance.

Note: This use of the comma is both for the sake of clarity and for a breathing pause. If you will read the examples again, you will find yourself pausing, quite naturally, at the comma. Thus, in the first sentence, you will read, "Although it was nearly noon," then a slight pause before finishing with: "the sky was overcast and dark." (This grammatical pause is much akin to the short pause in music, often used as a breathing respite.)

PRINCIPLE FOUR

Long introductory phrases are set off by commas.

Examples:

> *Looking at the facts behind the slick,* political talk (long introductory phrase)**,** we can see that the candidate has little to recommend him (main clause).

Note: Almost without exception, introductory phrases, *whether long or short,* that contain a participle or infinitive are set off by commas.

> *To bring about an amicable settlement,* one must use not only intelligence, but also prudence and patience.
>
> *Disappointed,* he fell back into his old slovenly ways.

Note: Even though *disappointed* does not qualify as a phrase, still it is a participle and clarity suggests the comma.

> *Having been a teacher for years,* I can tell you that most students are willing to learn.
>
> *After the lecture of confused statements and ill-timed jokes,* the students were in no gracious mood.

Note: This introductory phrase does not contain a verbal, but it is long enough to warrant a comma. Again, clarity and pause for breath are the motivating reasons.

EXERCISE III

Insert all the commas needed in the following sentences, explaining your use in every case.

1. Long hair beards and bare feet were generally the occasion for mockery among many although religion teaches us not to judge from appearances.

2. Not only were distinctive social and cultural innovations common in the sixties but many groups of people remained as conservative as ever.

3. We must not be surprised when we meet with bitterness hatred and prejudice for that has been the story of the human race.

4. We who still take the trouble to think must remain proud of JFK RFK and Martin Luther King for many years from now they will still be honored as remarkable men.

5. Younger persons are torn between violence and euphoria yet they remain fundamentally generous and dedicated.

6. Many dreams have been busted for we have seen indifference and selfishness all around us.

7. Yes I can understand that she amuses you but to let her stroke you kiss your hair and befriend you is hardly in your line.

8. To begin with a goal to strive without fear to end only after persistent struggle are the marks of a hero.

9. In his conversations with invited dissidents at his famous background briefings for the press and in private talks with reporters and com-

mentators Victor takes the greatest care to conceal any differences that may exist between him and the President.

10. When her horse Shane bucked Diane panicked was thrown to the ground broke her jaw and passed out.

PRINCIPLE FIVE

Set off non-restrictive clauses, words, and phrases with commas.

An element is considered *restrictive* only if it is essential to the definition or identification of the element it modifies. However, a *non-restrictive* element can be removed without loss of an important, identifying part of the meaning.

Example: a restrictive clause.

All the students *who study* will pass.

Explanation: The clause *who study* is restrictive; *only* those students who study will pass. If one takes the clause out, the sentence reads:

All the students will pass.

Obviously, this is incorrect.

Example A: a non-restrictive clause

Evelyn Mosser, *who was wearing a red dress* (non-restrictive clause), killed Ed Schultz. (The words not italicized contain all that is necessary for definition and identification of the subject.)

Example B: a restrictive clause

The woman *who was wearing a red dress* (restrictive clause) killed Ed Schultz. (The words not italicized are insufficient for complete definition and identification.)

Explanation: In sentence *A* the killer is identified by her name; *who was wearing a red dress* is therefore merely descriptive or not restrictive since presumably there is only one Evelyn Mosser.

In sentence *B* the killer is not identified by name. Who among all the women present killed her husband? The sentence in effect answers: not the one wearing the green dress, nor the one wearing the blue dress, but the one wearing the red dress. The clause, accordingly, is restrictive or essential to complete definition and identification.

Example A: a non-restrictive clause

All the villagers, *who are Republicans* (not necessary to identify the subject), will vote for Armstrong. (In other words, *all* the villagers are Republicans.)

Example B: a restrictive clause

All the villagers *who are Republicans* (necessary to define and identify the subject) will vote for Armstrong. (In other words, not all the villagers are Republicans, and only those who are voted for Armstrong.)

Explanation: In sentence *A* all the villagers are Republican; all will vote for Armstrong.

In sentence *B* not all the villagers are Republicans; only those who are, not the Democrats, will vote for Armstrong.

Examples:

(restrictive name) The novelist Dickens wrote rapidly.

(non-restrictive title) Dickens, *the novelist,* wrote rapidly.

Explanation: In the first sentence we restrict the meaning of *novelist* to this particular man: Dickens.

In the second sentence it is not necessary to restrict the name to make the specific identification. (The non-restrictive phrase helps classify Dickens among novelists, but it does not identify him.)

Examples:

(non-restrictive clause) All the girls, who were swimming, loved Jack.

(restrictive clause) All the girls *who were swimming* loved Jim.

Question: If both boys are on the same scene, who will have more girls to cope with, Jack or Jim? How can you tell? One boy, is loved by all the girls; the other is loved "only" by those engaged in a certain activity (i.e., swimming).

Example:

> When one considers, *for example,* how much time is wasted in useless oratory, he is not apt to be overjoyed by these conventions.

Example:

> The morning of June 17, 1970, *which was the most miserable morning in my life,* began innocently enough.

Example:

> My grandfather, *a man of remarkable strength,* often worked 12 hours a day.

Note: The non-restrictive element is in apposition.

Example:

> Dancing, *of course,* is forbidden.

Note: The non-restrictive element is parenthetical.

Examples:

> *Son,* mind your manners.
> How did you like her, *Father?*

Note: The non-restrictive elements are in direct address.

Other Uses of the Comma

1. *Numerals*   1,234,567.00

2. *Dates*   August 30, 1960, was . . . When only the month and year are given, a comma is optional: August, 1960 or August 1960. No commas are used when this less-used form appears: 30 August 1960.

3. *Addresses and geographical names* — 432 High Avenue, Clarksburg, Virginia, is . . .

4. *After the salutation in personal letters* — Dear Maurice,
(In business letters the salutation is followed by a colon.)

5. *To separate titles* — D. A. Phalen, Jr., admired . . .
Walter Hubbart, Ph.D., D.D., studied . . .

6. *For contrast* — I love Irene, not Penelope.

The Iroquois, not the Pawnees, were on the warpath.

7. *For clarity* — I speak not as an authority, but as an interested amateur.

After all, your shouting did no good. (To avoid reading: After all your shouting . . .)

What the cause is, is a matter of great concern.

When you can, do it.

I should do it now, and then forget about it. (To avoid reading: now and then)

8. *With quotation marks* (See unit below, "quotation marks.") — "When you see his uncontrollable anger," she said, "you too will be disturbed."

He turned and grunted, "Do what you please."

EXERCISE IV

Punctuate the following sentences. Explain in every case why you use commas as you do. Whenever a sentence can be punctuated in two ways, explain what difference in meaning the punctuation makes.

1. Lawrence's most sedulous critic Richard Aldington who in 1955 published a biographical inquiry into Lawrence's life maintained that he was a liar.

2. Lawrence of course invented himself; but Lowell Thomas who was then a young Princeton instructor made him a worldwide figure.

3. Lawrence protesting against the hero-worship he received through Thomas claimed that they had spent only a few days together—a statement which was probably true.

4. Lawrence when pressed for the truth about his life would laugh with glee.

5. In the end as we now know Lawrence himself no longer knew the difference between fact and fiction.

6. Aldington who punctured many legends about Lawrence's life points out that he could not have read more than 13,000 books.

7. Lawrence became famous for his journey his penchant for fancy dress his idiosyncrasies and zeal.

8. The British who were technically still at peace wanted a survey of the Egyptian-Turkish frontier a survey that Lawrence was able to give them.

9. The British had been dickering with the Sharif Hussein who was religious guardian of the Moslem holy places.

10. The revolt which became even more important after Turkey joined Germany in the war could have divided the Moslem world and indefinitely postponed progress in the Middle East.

11. While the girl who was most talented won the first prize, the girl who was most efficient won the second.

12. Howard Breman Jr. the mayor of Bristol often visited and spoke with the one who won second prize.

13. This second prize which was a one-way ticket to Bermuda was not appreciated although those who did not win it thought it was valuable.

14. You must find the person who is really guilty of the crime if you wish to release Ruth Gorman who you say is not guilty.

15. His lunch which consisted of tomato juice pork and beans coffee and crackers and cheese was not unusual.

16. His brother John Smith liked Jack Ready who was an ardent stereo enthusiast.

17. If you consider for example that all the models who work in New York are undernourished you begin to have your doubts about the profession's glamor.

18. Holmes often set out after a man who seemed to be guilty only to find later on that it was not he who was guilty but someone else whom he had not suspected.

19. Mr. Richards' position is not an easy one for he has persistently fallen into serious difficulties that threaten his security.

20. Apart from the fact that there is in existence a large body of Eliot criticism which means that future critics will be forced to go over familiar ground it is to be presumed or at least hoped that people who still read about Eliot's poetry will also have read the poetry itself.

21. Although the conduct of these men on Madison Avenue is not always excusable still we must admit that they are exceedingly clever advertisers.

22. It seems strange that critics of Congress who are supposedly intelligent men are often unwilling to acknowledge the many good things that come forth from that body.

23. Criticism is always easy especially if it is only of the negative variety but it is quite another thing to be positive and constructive in one's approach.

24. If these years are to be profitable ones they must be so through the advance of science if they are to be stirring ones then they can be so only through the advance of art.

The Comma Splice

A comma splice occurs when two independent clauses are improperly separated by a comma. This mistake must be particularly noted and avoided, not only because it leads to serious misreading, but also because it is so frequent. (Some teachers estimate that 20 percent of all mistakes in punctuating occur as a result of the comma splice.)

Remedies

1. Make two sentences and use the period.
2. Use the semicolon to make a compound sentence.
3. Make a compound sentence with a comma and coordinating conjunction.
4. Make one clause dependent.

Example:

He had, as usual, the best of intentions, however, he could not overcome the fatal temptation to have that first drink.	**comma splice**

Remedy 1.

He had, as usual, the best of intentions. *He* could not, however, overcome the fatal temptation to have that first drink.	**independent clauses changed into complete sentences**

Remedy 2.

He had, as usual, the best of intentions; however, he could not overcome the fatal temptation to have that first drink.	**semicolon erases comma splice by making a compound sentence**

Remedy 3.

He had usually the best of intentions, *but* he could not overcome the fatal temptation to have that first drink.	**independent clauses joined with comma and coordinating conjunction to make compound sentence**

Remedy 4.

Although he had, as usual, the best of intentions, he could not overcome the fatal temptation to have that first drink.	**first clause made dependent on second**

Example:

Tom Rumble came to English class on time, then he took a comfortable position and went to sleep.	**comma splice**

Remedy 1.

Tom Rumble came to English class on time. *Then* he took a comfortable position and went to sleep.	**two complete sentences**

Remedy 2.

Tom Rumble came to English class on time; then he took a comfortable position and went to sleep.	**semicolon**

Remedy 3.

Tom Rumble came to English class on time, *but* he took a comfortable position and went to sleep.	**conjunction plus comma**

Remedy 4.

When Tom Rumble came to English class on time, he took a comfortable position and went to sleep.	**first clause made dependent**

Example:

Two chapters have been covered in class, the third will have to be studied at home.	**comma splice**

Remedy 1.

Two chapters have been covered in class. *The* third will have to be studied at home.	**two complete sentences**

Remedy 2.

Two chapters have been covered in class; the third will have to be studied at home.	**semicolon**

Remedy 3.

Two chapters have been covered in class, *but* the third will have to be studied at home.	**conjunction plus comma**

Remedy 4.

Now that two chapters have been covered in class, the third will have to be studied at home.	**first clause made dependent**

comma—exercise

EXERCISE V

Correct the following sentences. Revise each in at least two ways.

1. Bagehot observed that in 1802 every hereditary monarch was insane, he prefaced this statement with the warning that it contained an approximation of truth.

2. *The Origin of Species* had an immediate success, the first edition was sold out on the first day of publication.

3. He was secretary to Washington, our first President, he was a literary man turned professional politician, one of the first we ever had.

4. The first two volumes are remarkable examples of what can be done, notes are few, but helpful and authoritative.

5. They never use primary sources, they use originals only for checking transcripts.

6. Dickens draws with the brush, heaps paint thickly, lets the line establish itself through contrast of masses of color, he is a thick artist, while Jane Austen is a thin one.

7. This interest in Hulme is not surprising, for in many ways he is still very much alive, his anti-romanticism is still current.

8. Mark Twain informed and taught succeeding generations of writers, nevertheless, after Franklin he seems to be the least understood of American writers.

9. The book begins with "Yankee Doodle" and ends with a gigantic index, the labor involved in collecting the information is staggering.

10. In the years before the war Haldane had two set-backs, the first was the refusal to make him Lord Chancellor.

EXERCISE VI

Correct sentences 1 to 4 by using the semicolon, 5 to 7 by making a compound sentence or by making two sentences out of one, 8 to 10 by making one clause dependent.

1. Many experts may not view their work lightly, their attitude, however, tends to convey this impression.

2. People in cities become anonymous, they lose that personal relationship of small towns.

3. Men, women, and children must respect, honor, and appreciate one another, they will only then learn what social well-being means.

4. The plot begins to thicken, Mr. Dycke appears, only to be duly shot by the landlady.

---

5. Journeys to the moon are exciting adventures, many people in the seventies, nevertheless, continue to question their practical value.

6. California remains a state of space, excitement, and unrest, Florida suggests tranquillity and dreams.

7. If you are bored with a movie, you can amuse yourself by watching the audience, you will find all sorts of reactions.

---

8. Tom made good grades in the first semester, in the second he began to coast and his grades went down.

9. The cattle began to grow restless late at night, the cowboys had a difficult time keeping them under control.

10. Irene often wished to stay out late at night, however, the thought of her father's anger was always a restraining influence.

EXERCISE VII

Correct the punctuation in the following sentences. Eliminate fragments by combining them with an independent clause or by making them complete sentences. (Cf. "the sentence," pp. 8–10)

1. The President of Yale did not recognize the renowned Shakespearean scholar until it was too late to greet him with proper respect. Mr. Kittredge, who had taught for many years at Harvard.

2. George's conduct was often unpredictable because eccentric. For example, his habit of coming late for dinner and his constant interruption of conversation.

3. Because time is running short and I am extremely tired this evening. I shall close now and try to write a longer letter later in the week when I feel more energetic.

4. Patriotism spreads from the home to the community. From the community to the state and from the state to the nation.

5. The dean asked me to write this article. Not only because of my misconduct but also because I was the first student he could use as an example for others.

6. The destruction of the church brought back many memories. Of brides given to grooms, of babies in their baptismal dress, of relatives mourning the dead. Some pleasant occasions, others saddening.

7. Edmund took great delight in walking through the woods. Dressed in faded clothes and boots that were much too big for him. A boy with boundless energy and high imagination. But impractical and unreliable.

8. He had good intentions but a weak will. Whenever he found an opportunity to steal with only a remote chance of being caught.

9. No snow in either December or January. What a winter for skiing.

10. The glory that was Greece is gone. Nor can we experience the grandeur of Rome.

11. One spectator jeered the umpire constantly. The umpire who was trying his best to be impartial and was really doing a creditable job.

12. The performance is nearing the end, and you see a small girl in the front row. Crying because the end is so sad.

The Semicolon

PRINCIPLE ONE

"Commas within, semicolon between." That is, if you have commas *within*

1. independent clauses
2. dependent clauses
3. phrases of a series,

then use a semicolon *between* them.

Example 1. semicolon between independent clauses

Gloria Ziegenfus tried to appear sophisticated by wearing gaudy clothes, applying heavy mascara, and tinting her hair; but she succeeded only in making herself look ridiculous.

Explanation: The commas after *clothes* and *mascara* separate items of a series within the first independent clause. A comma, as a consequence, would be too weak to separate the two major parts of the sentence (the two independent clauses). A semicolon neatly distinguishes a major separation (between the clauses) from a minor separation (between items of a series).

Note what happens when the series is omitted:

> Gloria tried to appear sophisticated, but she succeeded only in making herself look ridiculous.

Here only a comma is necessary to separate the two main clauses. (See Principle Three under "Main Uses of the Comma," p. 22.)

Example 2. semicolon between dependent clauses

> We all know that Aaron committed many crimes, such as robberies, arson, assault, and the like; that he has been resolutely untrustworthy, shiftless, and callow; and, finally, that he shows no evidence of wishing to reform.

Explanation: We have here three noun clauses, all of which begin with the conjunction *that,* and all of which are the object of the verb *know.* Note that there are commas within all three noun clauses separating items in a series and an appositive (*finally*). We accordingly use the semicolon to mark clearly the break between noun clauses.

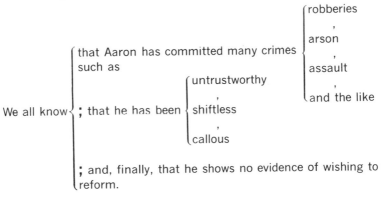

Example 3. semicolon between items in a series when the items contain internal punctuation

The following legislators were named to the Committee on Civil Rights: Senator Longhorn, Austin, Texas, Democrat; Senator George Keever, Beatty, Pennsylvania, Democrat; and Representative William Hook, Hoboken, Indiana, Republican.

Explanation: Here we have a list of three men. There are commas within each part of the series or list, separating each name from place of origin and party affiliation. Semicolons are needed to keep the items in the series distinct from each other.

The following legislators were named to the committee:
{
Senator Longhorn,
from Austin, Texas,
party Democrat
;Senator George Keever
from Beatty, Pennsylvania
party Democrat
; Representative Wm. Hook,
from Hoboken, Indiana,
party Republican.
}

PRINCIPLE TWO

Use a semicolon between two independent clauses not joined by a conjunction.

Examples:

He began by stealing; he died stealing.

All pleasures were the same to him; everything left him jaded and disgruntled.

Joe Steep is a man of integrity; he is completely unselfish; he is vehemently patriotic.

Note the difference when a conjunction is added to these sentences:

He began by stealing and he died stealing.

All pleasures were the same to him, because everything left him jaded and disgruntled.

PRINCIPLE THREE

Use a semicolon between two independent clauses joined by any one of the following conjunctive adverbs: *accordingly, consequently, furthermore, hence, still, however, moreover, nevertheless, otherwise, therefore.*

Examples:

He has worked long hours and suffered much; nevertheless, he has retained his health and good spirits.

As a matter of policy I refuse to accept the presidency; however, I might accept under certain circumstances.

Joe Speck is a brute, a cad, a snob, a simpleton; still some people consider him a gentleman.

He must have finished his assignments; otherwise he would not have passed the course.

Note: Because these conjunctive adverbs are usually set off by commas, the commas within the clauses would also dictate a semicolon between.

Note: A semicolon must separate items of parallel structure; independent and independent clause, dependent and dependent clause, phrase and phrase. *Do not,* for instance, separate an independent from a dependent clause or a clause from a phrase by means of a semicolon.

Wrong: Hardy would begin, surely, with his massed chorus of the Pities, Irony, The Years, and the rest looking down the corridors of time; where fate had spread its traps of doom and gloom.

Explanation: The last clause is dependent and is incorrectly separated from the clause upon which it depends.

Note: Do not associate a semicolon with a colon. It is not a half colon even though its name seems to suggest this. See use of the colon, pp. 40.

FURTHER EXAMPLES OF SEMICOLON

1. The captain orders every grain of wheat destroyed; nothing but the weapons of war can be preserved.

   two independent clauses not connected by a conjunction

2. The captain orders that not a goat, ox,

   commas separating items in series

   or cow can be left alive; but all horses, capable men, and weapons must be preserved.

   semicolon separating two independent clauses that have internal punctuation

3. One chapter discusses local words for horses; another describes a village

   semicolon separating first two independent clauses. No conjunction

   occasion, or pageant; a third concerns diseases and the expressions used to describe them.

   semicolon separating second and third independent clauses. No conjunction

4. Its three main divisions deal with the Sumerians, the Babylonians, and the Egyptians, who are called the "Components"; the Hittites and Hurrians, and the Israelites, who are called the "Catalysts"; and the Persians, who are called the "Synthesizers."

   items in minor series separated by commas

   items in the larger of major series separated by semicolons

5. Use a semicolon between two independent clauses not already separated or joined by a conjunction; ordinarily use a comma when a conjunction is used.

   two rules are expressed in this sentence; one is put into use.

Formulas for the Semicolon—Almost always (at least nine out of ten times) when a semicolon is used, it is for the sake of separating independent clauses. Its use can be expressed in this manner:

sentence one: *indep. clause, internal punctuation; indep. clause.*
sentence two: *indep. clause; (no conjunction) indep. clause.*
sentence three: *indep. clause; (conjunctive adverb) indep. clause.*

EXERCISE VIII

In the following sentences insert all the semicolons needed. In each case explain why you use the mark. If certain sentences do not need a semicolon, explain why not.

1. This description may be widened, the basic social, cultural and economic needs of young people, GI's, and many other large groups, are not being met.

2. The study also showed that the time lag between discovery and broad social or intellectual impact is constantly shrinking, it is now about ten to 15 years, a period similar to that for breakthroughs in technology.

3. A chicken will eat more in the presence of another chicken than it will in isolation, it will similarly eat more when it is keeping company with a mirror.

4. When you go to the store, you must remember to order these items: two steaks, one inch thick, about a pound apiece, two heads of lettuce, cottage cheese, the large curd, two dozen eggs, and some cauliflower, fresh, not the frozen.

5. He had been, so he said, a desperate rebel, but he hoped eventually to be a conformist.

6. Nobody seemed to consider that he was now alone after forty years, his friends estranged, his children abroad, his wife dead, that he was lonely and starved for affection, that he could adjust to his new situation only with agonizing difficulty.

7. Cardinal Flanagan promised them 15 minutes, but then talked with them for two hours, he offered to make every effort to keep the schools open.

8. Unless we have prudence we cannot survive, unless we have love we cannot enjoy.

9. Love is patient and kind, love is not jealous or boastful, it is not arrogant or rude. Love does not insist on its own way, it is not irritable or resentful, it does not rejoice at wrong, it bears all things, believes all things, hopes all things, it never ends.

10. In 1969, Bougla Transport supported the Opera with a gift of $135,000, three years later Echo Air Lines followed by contributing $500,000.

EXERCISE IX

Join the following groups of simple sentences into one compound or one compound-complex sentence. In each sentence use a semicolon, explaining why you have done so. You may add or change words.

1. Excellence in teaching and scholary activity are of prime importance in faculty evaluation. It is recognized that other activities, such as administrative and committee contributions to the college or community activity, also may be considered in the evaluation.

2. Irene kept igniting him. Looking back, he could remember the times he actually caught fire.

3. Student interest at Mermian U. in curriculum is innovation is being tested. It carries forward his interest in liberating students from the restrictions of credits, fragmented courses, rigid schedules, examinations, the semester system calendar and other practices.

4. A word, once spoken, cannot be recalled. It is forever gone.

5. He cares little for money. He has earned much and spent much.

6. Some may feel that they have succeeded in manipulating or dominating the authorities. These people do not have the foresight to see the effects of their work.

7. Students no longer will accept the shoddy, poor, lifeless dregs of undergraduate life. They are demanding much more, a professionalism based on a need to be the best.

8. The so-called ivory towers of academe are gone. Life—real life, virile life, the life of action and policy-shaping thought—has moved in.

9. A democracy, no less that any other form of society, must foster excellence if it is to survive. It should not allow the emotional scars of old battles to confuse it on this point.

10. The Turkish astronomer presented his discovery to Congress. He was in Turkish dress. So nobody would believe what he said.

The Colon

PRINCIPLE

The colon is a mark of punctuation that formally introduces
1. an explanation
2. an amplification
3. a series
4. a long quotation

Often it is to grammar what equal marks ($=$) are to mathematics. Or, it is almost equivalent to saying "that is."

---

1. The sudden change in mood did not surprise John: he had been warned to expect it.

colon to introduce a clause of explanation

Note: Here the colon introduces a second statement that explains the first. In effect, the colon says this: John was not surprised because of a previous warning.

Variation: The sudden change in mood did not surprise John, for he had been warned to expect it.

2. There are many signs of bad taste in America: some you will find in our movies, others in television, and still others in our churches.

colon to introduce amplifying examples

Note: Here the colon introduces formally an expansion or amplification of the first statement about the presence of bad taste.

3. The reasons for his expulsion are the following: he has been incompetent from the very beginning, he has steadfastly refused to apply himself, and he has been consistently unreliable.

colon for introduction—It acts as a formal introduction to a series of reasons.

4. Plot to Coleridge did not mean the mere story or fable, but organic structure, and the way in which one scene contains in it the seed from which all that follows grows: "All is growth, evolution, *genesis*, each line, each word almost begets the following."

colon for proof—The quotation of Coleridge supports the opening statement; the colon leads the reader to expect some such support for a statement that will not be accepted by everyone.

5. Over the bar was printed a notice: Work is the curse of the drinking class.

colon for introduction to saying

Note: Although the colon is a valuable mark of punctuation, one should not overuse it. Remember that it is a formal mark of introduction. It should not be substituted for a semicolon when a semicolon is capable of handling the situation.

Dashes, Parentheses, Brackets

PRINCIPLE

There are various ways of setting off parenthetical material within a sentence. Each way creates a different effect. Dashes emphasize. Parentheses minimize. Commas enclose.

Example A:

Most college coeds— if they have even a grain of intelligence—will realize that men do not marry girls who think.

material emphasized

Example B:

Sooner or later (since everything that is possible seems to happen) this respect for tradition was bound to be challenged.

material minimized

Example C:

> The good that men do, Mr. Shake-   **material enclosed**
> speare reminds us, is often interred
> with their bones.

Explanation: In each of the three sentences we have parenthetical material set off from the rest of the sentence. The dashes in *Example A* stress or highlight the parenthetical material. They thereby lend a certain prominence to the clause.

The parentheses in *Example B* do not give such prominence to the enclosed material. Actually the parenthetical material is incidental and the sentence sense remains much the same after the *since* clause is removed.

The commas in *Example C* keep the parenthetical material within the sentence without giving the force that a dash would or cutting it off from the rest of the sentence as parentheses would.

Note: It is frequently difficult for both writer and reader to determine the subtle distinction between dashes and parentheses. When does one emphasize, and when de-emphasize? Although the distinction is fine, and to some picayune, it is good not to lose sight of it altogether.

1. The Dash (two hyphens on the typewriter) is used as follows:

1. when there is a sudden break in the sentence
2. when emphasis is placed on the parenthetical material
3. when there is internal punctuation in the parenthetical material
4. when the parenthetical material demands punctuation at the end, such as a question mark, quotation mark, or exclamation.

Example 1:

> The new queen of National Snowflake
> Week—we remember how scrawny   **for a sudden break**
> she was when small—beamed celes-
> tial satisfaction.

Example 2:

> No one—except the fool and the
> pedant—believes that he can become   **for emphasis**
> an outstanding writer by paying at-
> tention only to punctuation.

parentheses—brackets

Example 3:

Many scientific advances—in Italy, in Germany, in France, but not in Spain—have helped to raise the general standard of living in Europe.

for parenthetical material that has internal punctuation

Example 4:

The President—who can envy his position?—must deal with Russia almost every day.

for end punctuation

2. **Parentheses**—to set off material that is incidental and that will not fit easily into the grammatical structure of the sentence.

Example:

The painting "Boors' Carouse" was painted by D. Teniers the younger. (He is considered by many to be the greatest of the Flemish Painters.) In 1970 it was worth well over a hundred thousand dollars.

interrupting sentence or clause set off

Example:

In *The Manner Is Ordinary* (first published as an Image Book in 1957) Father LaFarge states that nothing short of a gospel of limitless love can convert the world.

parentheses minimize interrupting modifier

3. **Brackets**—used to enclose personal or editorial comment within a direct quotation.

Example:

In "The Pleasures of Music" Aaron Copland asks, "What is it that makes his [Bach's] finest scores so profoundly moving?"

reference missing in quotation supplied

Explanation: The writer supplies *Bach's,* which is not in the original sentence as written by Copland. This insertion is necessary to make clear the antecedent of *his*.

Example:

> I was tempted to disagree with his last statement: "This period [from 1789 to 1850] was marked by a steady aversion to rococo art (as many authors term it)."

missing reference supplied parenthetical remark quoted

Explanation: From 1789 to 1850 is inserted by the writer who cites the quotation; *as many authors term it* is part of the original quotation.

Example:

> In 1763 Robert Corrington wrote: "Their [sic] are two ways to get to church on time."

irregularity in quotation noted

Explanation: Sic (Latin for "thus") is inserted to make clear that Corrington is being quoted exactly. In other words, blame Corrington for the misspelling.

Quotation Marks

The proper use of quotation marks can be shown best by examples.

1. "A great deal of nonsense is being written in England at this time," Edith Sitwell said, "for modern poets and the reading public are out of touch with each other, and take no interest in each other."

explanatory material divides the quotation; note position of commas and periods are always placed inside the quotation marks

2. It was called "protective custody"; however, the refugees were treated with unusual violence.

semicolons are always placed outside the quotation marks

3. He asked, "What do you intend to do?"

the question mark is placed inside the quotation marks when the quotation is interrogative

quotation marks

4. Did he say, "I shall go to Europe this summer"?

the question mark is placed outside the quotation marks when the statement as a whole, but not the quotation, is interrogative

5. Did he ask, "What do you intend to do?"

when both the sentence as a whole and the quotation are interrogative, the question mark goes inside.

Note: It is never necessary to duplicate terminal punctuation (periods, question marks, exclamation marks).

Note: The exclamation mark and the dash follow the same practice as the question mark in regard to their place inside or outside the quotation marks.

6. The Apostle said, "Lord. it is good for us to be here."

a short quotation is formally introduced by a comma

7. Jack Benny's "Well!" has become famous in show business.

a short emphatic quotation needs no introductory punctuation

8. Jacques Barzun says: "The term 'humanities,' descended from the Renaissance catch phrase, litterae humaniores, can be appealed to as carrying the suggestion of 'peculiarly human,' but it is mere suggestion, not proof."

a long quotation is formally introduced by a colon when elements within the direct quotation demand quotation marks, alternate between double and single quotation marks

9. Only three days ago the defendant made this statement: "Judge, I heard her say, 'I'll kill him if he ever returns.'"

the main quotation set off by double marks quotation within quotation set off by singles

Note: Do not use quotation marks for indirect quotations.

10. He said, "I am willing to pay for the damage I have caused."

direct quotation; notice change to first person in quotation

quotations, parentheses—exercise 47

He said *that he was willing to pay for the damage he had caused.*	indirect quotation; notice use of third person throughout

11. "You have not forgotten how you walked with the poor lady on that hot day?" asked Clym.
    "No," said the boy.
    "And what she said to you?"
    "No."
	As a rule, in recording conversation, consider each change of speaker a new paragraph.

Note: If an unbroken quotation continues over several paragraphs, use quotation marks at the beginning of each paragraph, but closing quotation marks only at the end of the quotation.

12. G. M. Hopkins' "Pied Beauty"	quotation marks for brief poems not published under their own title (underline poems published under their own title, e.g., Paradise Lost).
13. "The Black Forest," *Holiday,* by Wechsberg	quotation marks for articles
14. the chapter "Checking Out" in *Bears in the Caviar* by Charles Thayer	quotation marks for parts of larger works
15. "First Confession" by Frank O'Connor	quotation marks for short stories

EXERCISE X*

Punctuate all the parenthetical and quoted material in the following sentences. In each case of parenthetical material please explain why you use one method of punctuation in preference to the other two.

1. The subject of their discourse a young clever man was coming into that heath from of all contrasting places in the world Paris.

2. Don't scratch your face said her aunt. Will you walk with me to meet him this evening?

*All sentences in this exercise adapted from Thomas Hardy's *The Return of the Native.*

3. I hear that I will never be happy she said. How can you say I am happy and nothing is changed.

4. His daily life it was of a curious microscopic sort was limited to a circuit of a few feet. His familiar companions believe me were bees and butterflies.

5. What do you propose to do? said Eustasia. You seem to take a very milk interest in what I propose, said Clym. You mistake me, she answered, reviving at his reproach. I am only thinking. He asked, What of? Excuse me, she replied, I was distracted. Did I hear you say What of? Or did you say, I'm tired?

6. Four hours after the present time that is at midnight he was to be ready to drive her to Budmouth.

7. There on the outside of the quilt have you ever seen one quite like it? was the impression of her form, showing that the bed had not been opened; and what was more significant she had not taken her candlestick downstairs.

8. To fly as his mistress and she knew that he loved her was of the nature of humiliation. Any one who had stood by now would have pitied her not so much on account of her exposure to weather but for that other form of misery denoted by the rocking movement that her feelings once so different now imparted.

9. As the evening advanced the wind was rasping and scraping at the corners of the house he walked restlessly about the rooms. Who's there he cried when he heard a subdued hiss under the downpour. O Clym, come down and let me in.

10. Thomasin being left alone took off some of her wet garments and carried the baby born only recently to Clym's bed.

Italics

In typed or hand-written manuscripts italics are indicated by underlining.

Examples:

1. *You* is misused in your last sentence. Remember to cross your *t's*.

   words used as words, letters used as letters are italicized

2. The *S. S. Leonardo da Vinci* made its maiden voyage in July 1960.

names of ships are italicized

3. Among his possessions were a recent issue of *Commonweal, Romeo and Juliet* and Virginia Woolf's *The Common Reader.*

titles of magazines, plays, and books are italicized

4. Have you seen Michelangelo's *The Conversion of Saint Paul?*

titles of works of art are italicized

5. She was famous for her rendition of *Caro Nome* in *Rigoletto.*

titles of musical selections and operas are italicized.

6. He was instructed to act *sub rosa.*

foreign words or expressions not yet naturalized are italicized

7. You don't mean that *she* did it?

emphasis can be given to certain words or phrases by italicizing them—DO NOT OVERUSE THIS DEVICE

Note: Do not use italics or quotation marks to indicate slang or other substandard expressions. If the writer feels that the expressions will not be recognized as slang or substandard, then he should not use them. Avoid doing this: He was looking "sharp" all right. He bumped into the *hippie* on one of those "blue Monday" days.

The Apostrophe

Use the apostrophe plus s to form the possessive singular of all nouns and the possessive plural of all those nouns not ending in s.

woman's role   Mary's birthday
women's role   children's recreation

Use the apostrophe alone to form the possessive of plural nouns ending in s.

>   wolves' clothing   Smiths' house
>   girls' dresses   Joneses' parties

Use the apostrophe plus s to form the possessive singular of indefinite pronouns.

>   one's liberty   another's attempt

Apostrophe indicates the omission of a letter or number.

>   isn't   o'clock   O'Toole   the summer of '62

Use apostrophe and s to form the plural of letters, numbers, and words used as words.

>   your *p*'s and *q*'s
>   They came in *2*'s and *3*'s.
>   There are too many *the*'s in the line.

Note the following:

>   it's (contraction of it is)
>   its (no contraction, but the possessive of it)
>   Moses' life   Orestes' tribulation
>   father-in-law's rights
>   mothers-in-law's possessiveness
>   hers, yours, ours, theirs
>   conscience' sake (addition of another s would result in three sibilants)
>   University of Kansas' football team

Note: In forming the possessive, try to avoid an unnecessary and unpronounceable duplication of sound. Thus: Orestes' tribulation, not Orestes's tribulation; conscience' sake, not conscience's sake.

A Miscellany in Punctuation

1. **Ellipsis**—The ellipsis (. . .) indicates that some part of the quoted material or thought has been deleted.

Example:

> "When . . . it becomes necessary for one people to dissolve the political bands which have connected them with another . . . a decent respect to the opinions of mankind requires that they should declare the causes which impel them to the separation."

Note: The ellipsis is always shown by three dots or periods, never more, never less. However, if the ellipsis occurs at the end of a sentence, then the period ending that sentence must not be omitted.

Example:

> "My friends: No one, not in my situation, can appreciate my feeling of sadness at this parting. . . ."

Note: We have here a period designating the end of a quoted sentence and three dots or periods denoting ellipsis.

Example:

> I was about to reprimand him in public, but . . .

Note: Ellipsis indicates an interruption of thought, a decision not to continue with what is apparent or a loss of thought sequence.

2. Capitals

A. A short, complete sentence after a colon need not be capitalized; if, however, it is a long, complete sentence, capitalize it.

Examples:

> He ignored her solicitation: what else could he have done?

> The concept turns out to be an old one: If you strive earnestly, work diligently, and utilize your talents properly, you will succeed in time.

B. Do not capitalize names of seasons: spring, autumn, summer, winter.

C. Capitalize *North, South, East* and *West* when they refer to a definite section of the country.

Examples:

> He was a typical native of the South.
> He decided to change his luck by traveling north.

D. Capitalize names of relatives when they are used as proper names.

Examples:

> He visited with his Aunt Mary, but he did not visit all his aunts.
> I left the matter up to Father. (Out of courtesy, names for members of one's family, when used formally, are capitalized.)

3. Hyphen—Note the difference between a hyphen (-) and a dash (—).

Example:

You can expect to have certainty about this in only one	**hyphen indicates syllabic division at the end of a line**
place—in heaven.	**dash (a double hyphen on the typewriter) indicates sharp turn of thought**

A. Two words used together, especially if one is a noun, and modifying a noun are hyphenated.

two-lane highway	a well-balanced mind
a hundred-foot tower	a second-class citizen
a clear-eyed young man	slow-moving merchandise

B. Hyphenate numerals from twenty-one to ninety-nine and fractions.

fifty-five	seventy-eight	sixty-two
three-fourths	one-eighth	

C. In certain instances it is necessary to hyphenate in order to bring out a special meaning.

re-create (not *recreate*)   re-cover (not *recover*)

D. Hyphenate to avoid a double vowel or triple consonant.

re-educate   re-employ   pre-existent
bell-like

But: co-operate *or* cooperate   co-ordinate *or* coordinate

E. Hyphenate between a prefix and a proper name.

pre-Reformation   post-Truman   ex-President Johnson

F. Hyphenate after the prefixes *ex-* and *self-*.

ex-wife   self-propelled   ex-congressman
self-taught

4. **Exclamation Mark (!)**—Do not overuse, and never use more than one at one time. Therefore, avoid such expressions as: "She is beautiful!" (This is grammatically correct, but the mark is unnecessary.) "What a dream!!" "I could have danced all night!!!" "Bang!!!!" "Oh, it's you!!!" (The tendency to use many dashes and a multitude of exclamation marks is regarded by some as feministic. Perhaps this is because, according to one view, many women believe everything they say is either by way of a tangent or of startling importance.)

EXERCISE XI

Correct all errors in punctuation in the following sentences. Supply any marks of punctuation that are needed.

1. A recent review of "Hedda Gabler" [by Ibsen] states "that Hedda presents a problem to men." She is so the magazine goes on to say: "a woman with a strong masculine component . . .," She cherishes her father's pistols and uses them. "As a very young woman, Hedda had been a kind of platonic muse to Eilert Lovborg . . ." She is married to Jorgen Tesman, a pedant "Out of temperamental fatigue (I have danced practically all my life—and I was getting tired . . . My summer was up") . . ."

2. "There are innumerable types of threshold interest which bring readers to fiction.", Brooks and Warren tell us in their book "The Scope of

Fiction''. They point out, ''There are ''sports'' stories, ''young'' love stories, ''marriage love'' stories, . . . ''Wild West'' stories, . . . and the like.'' Whether a reader of fiction expects ''a high degree of fidelity to the external facts. . .'' or expects ''the pleasure of escape'' depends upon a variety of factors, one of them being his interests in life.

3. On a rainy afternoon at six thirty two Joseph—returning from his house–to–house survey—noticed a copy of Dickens' ''David Copperfield'' in the display-window of a book-store. What a beautiful binding it had! He entered the store and asked the price of the bald pated proprietor: but he learned that it was much too expensive. He decided *immediately* that despite it's beautiful binding the book would have to remain in the store-window.

4. The Joneses budget was in good shape in the 50s, so they decided to take a trip abroad. After buying tickets for the ''Queen Mary,'' they applied for their passport and began to take the *inevitable* shots; shots against this, shots against that. For a while they decided that they ''had had it,'' as the saying goes. But they were ''game'' and finally everything was in readiness. You only live once was their motto.

5. It is estimated that two thirds of all drivers despise three lane highways. Some highway engineers should be reemployed as traveling salesmen or truck drivers; they would soon learn that any safety minded American would not construct this kind of road. Its usefulness belongs to the pre Teddy Roosevelt days when there was not the overflow of traffic there is today.

6. There are many reasons for his disturbance; for one thing, his ex wife continually writes threatening letters, for another, he lost his job on the Lincoln highway project. In many ways, he feels he is a first class heel. At times he wishes he could recreate his past, avoiding those mistakes he so much deplores now that its too late. He knows now that, if he had minded his ps and qs when he was young, he would not be a ''thorn'' in his childrens' side.

SENTENCE SENSE

Modifiers

PRINCIPLE

Place modifiers as close as possible to the word modified. There are three serious kinds of mistakes in this regard:

1. The misplaced modifier
2. The squinting modifier
3. The dangling modifier

---

1. Misplaced Modifier

Example: (In this and following examples, defective modifiers are italicized.)

Grace gave the statue to a friend *that was made of plaster.*

clause modifies "statue" and must be placed next to it

Revisions:

Grace gave a friend the statue that was made of plaster.

Grace gave the plaster statue to a friend.

Example:

He had only two dollars.

Observe the differences in meaning caused by shifting the placement of the word *only.*

a. Only Gary hit his cousin on the nose.
b. Gary only hit his cousin on the nose.
c. Gary hit only his cousin on the nose.
d. Gary hit his only cousin on the nose.
e. Gary hit his cousin only on the nose.
f. Gary hit his cousin on his only nose.
g. Gary hit his cousin on the nose only.

Note: The above seven sentences make a point; but do not take the point too scrupulously, for many times the meaning is clear even when the *only* is technically in the wrong place. Thus hardly anyone would quibble over this sentence: "He only wanted two dollars." To insist on placing *only* before *two* is petty.

The defective modifiers italicized below would give improbable or impossible meanings unless revised. Markers show placement of the modifier in possible revision.

Examples:

1. He *nearly went* ∧ half the distance to the goal.

   "nearly" probably does not modify "went"

2. John should learn ∧ whatever is demanded *quickly*.

   "quickly" modifies "should learn"

3. I ∧ prefer to *always* read Dickens during winter.

   "always" is better as a modifier for "prefer"

Note: Many formal writers try to avoid splitting the two elements of an infinitive with a modifier, although the anathema against a split infinite is not as binding as it used to be.

4. ∧ The Cadillac ∧ was stalled on the turnpike *out of gas*.

   "out of gas" modifies "Cadillac"

5. The operation was performed ∧ before much harm was done *by the surgeon*.

   "by the surgeon" modifies "was performed"

6. Every evening ∧ Rubenstein ∧ played the piano *on a highly polished bench*.

   "on . . . bench" modifies "Rubenstein"

7. *Not being able to write a complete sentence,* Mr. Plockett was forced to fail the student ∧.

   presumably "not being able to . . ." modifies "student"

   Mr. Plockett failed the student who was not able . . .

   revision recasts phrase modifier, making a clause

8. ∧ He kept a diary ∧ of all the girls he had kissed *in his desk drawer*.

   a tight squeeze unless modifier is detached from verb "kissed"

9. ∧ There was one course ∧ that taught how to make atom bombs *at Westmont State College.*   **an explosive situation unless modifier is detached from the infinitive "to make"**

2. **Squinting Modifier**—a modifier that does not clearly modify one specific part of the sentence, or one that seems to modify two parts. Correct the squinting modifier by moving it to a place that will eliminate vagueness or ambiguity.

Examples:

A. The conductor announced *when it was nine o'clock* the train would stop.

    Ambiguity:
    Did the conductor announce this at nine o'clock?
    Or will the train stop at nine o'clock?

    Revisions:
    When it was nine o'clock, the conductor announced that the train would stop.
    The conductor announced that the train would stop at nine o'clock.

B. The trooper who was ∧ pushed *unintentionally* shot the boy ∧. (Markers show placement of modifier for possible revision.)

C. ∧ He promised his mother *after the game* he would empty the garbage ∧.

D. ∧ Players who strike out *in four cases out of five* should be traded by the Mets.

    Revisions:
    In four cases out of five players who strike out . . .

    The Mets should trade any player who strikes out in four cases out of five.

3. **Dangling Modifier**—This is actually a contradiction in terms: a modifier that does not modify. Revise the sentence by finding a word it will modify.

Examples:

A. On entering the room, the dilatory students are quickly seen.

   Explanation: Entering has nothing in the sentence to modify. Correct the mistake by making the implicit subject explicit.

   Revision:
   Entering the room, the instructor sees the dilatory students.

B. Being thoroughly tired, the swim in the lake was a welcome relief.

   Revision:
   Being thoroughly tired, I welcomed the swim in the lake.

C. While at the movie, the school caught fire.

   Revision:
   While we were at the movie, the school caught fire.

D. When walking down the corridor, a huge number of books is cumbersome to me.

   Revision:
   When I am walking down the corridor . . .

   Explanation: Although the example sentence does mention a person (*me*), the modifier *when walking* . . . does not modify this word; it seems here to modify books. To avoid the Disneyesque absurdity of walking books, the sentence must supply a personal subject for *walking*.

   Note: Certain expressions have become idiomatic and absolute; they, therefore, do not demand an explicit subject, but may be said to modify the sentence's assertion as a whole.

   e.g., Generally speaking, this principle holds true at all conventions. Allowing for a certain small percentage of error, the estimate can be accepted as reliable.

EXERCISE XII

The sentences below contain modifiers that are misplaced or squinting or dangling. In each case correct the grammatical error.

1. Joanne decided early in September to be on the Dean's List.

2. Palmer saw the ball stop just short of the hole for another bogey, an eminently talented athlete with a disappointing season.

3. At the age of five, her mother first put Gypsy Rose Lee on stage.

4. Pete kept a careful report on his brother's activities in the top drawer of his desk.

5. While trying to put the final touches to his inaugral address, the telephone rang.

6. Kittredge made it quite clear that Hamlet was not a victim of indecision on Monday.

7. Having bought our tickets to *La Traviata* two months in advance, our seats at the Met were a distinct disappointment.

8. Florence only drank Martinis at Christmastime; at other times she never drank anything stronger than Pepsi.

9. As a totally irresponsible student, the Dean dismissed the gifted, well-liked Sam Smetana.

10. Having glanced briefly at the current issue of *The New Republic,* the problem of Viet Nam was clear as far as Susan was concerned.

11. *West Side Story* was not in the least way monotonous, eating candy and holding hands with eagerness.

12. Traveling on the N.J. Turnpike, the many orchards of the state and magnificent stables of the state were impressive.

13. The Senator from Oklahoma urged his fellow senators to vote for the anti-pollution bill with copious tears in the process.

14. His English teacher made suggestions to the student for the next paper that was having trouble with punctuation.

15. Having fastened our seat belts, the jet landed within ten minutes.

16. With justifiable pride the dramatics teacher watched his students acting from the third row center.

17. He kept all his money in the Manhattan First National Bank that he had earned in the late sixties.

18. Jake was careful to explain what had happened at court to his fiancée.

19. The singer returned from professional life he had led to hate.

20. Jeremy had the list of 16 girls he had kissed in his diary.

Parallelism

PRINCIPLE

Parallel or equal ideas should be expressed by parallel or equal structure. When parallelism is called for, one idea, reference, part of speech, or grammatical structure must be balanced with an equal or equivalent element. The use of parallelism is another way to introduce ideas in a co-ordinate structure (cf. compound sentences).

Example A:

She liked dancing and to sing.

Explanation: Dancing and *to sing* are objects of the verb *liked.* They must be parallel in structure.

Correction:

She liked $\begin{cases} \text{\textit{dancing}} \\ \text{\textit{and}} \\ \text{\textit{singing.}} \end{cases}$ She liked $\begin{cases} \text{\textit{to dance}} \\ \text{\textit{and}} \\ \text{\textit{to sing.}} \end{cases}$

Better:

She liked to $\begin{cases} \text{\textit{dance}} \\ \text{\textit{and}} \\ \text{\textit{sing.}} \end{cases}$

Example B:

They debated whether they should stay in town or to make an effort to get back home.

Correction:

They debated whether to $\begin{cases} \text{\textit{stay in town}} \\ \text{\textit{or}} \\ \text{\textit{make an effort}} \\ \text{\textit{to get back.}} \end{cases}$

Note: It is always important to realize just where you should establish the parallel lines; in this sentence, for instance, do they come after *debated, whether, they,* or *should?* Wherever they come, what follows must be parallel and make complete sense. As a rule, draw the parallel lines as late in the sentence as possible in order to economize.

Note the difference in the economy of the following sentences:

Either {
‖you will be the hero
or
‖you will be the goat
}

Either you {
‖will be the hero
or
‖will be the goat
}

Either you will {
‖be the hero
or
‖be the goat
}

Either you will be {
‖the hero
or
‖the goat
}

Either you will be the {
‖hero
or
goat
}

Example C:

The painting was neither attractive nor was it enjoyable.

Correction:

The painting was neither {
‖*attractive*
nor
enjoyable
}

Note: Disjunctives (*not only . . . but also, neither . . . nor, either . . . or,*) demand parallelism in structure. In this case, the parallel structure is set up after *neither,* and elements preceding *neither* should not be made part of the parallel structure.

Example D:

Dorothy was not only undernourished but also had a bad temper.

Correction:

Dorothy was not only $\left\{\begin{array}{l}\text{undernourished} \\ \text{but also} \\ \textit{ill-tempered.}\end{array}\right.$

Example E:

Either you will study or fail the course.

Correction:

You will either $\left\{\begin{array}{l}\textit{study} \\ \textit{or} \\ \textit{fail the course.}\end{array}\right.$

Example F:

The teacher was shrewd and being too keen to be fooled.

Correction:

The teacher was too $\left\{\begin{array}{l}\text{shrewd} \\ \text{and} \\ \text{keen}\end{array}\right\}$ to be fooled.

Example G:

His education, unlike most students, did not end when he graduated.

Correction:

unlike $\left\{\begin{array}{l}\text{His education} \\ \text{that of most students}\end{array}\right\}$ did not end when he graduated.

Note: In this parallel structure, the noun *education* needs to be balanced by its equivalent, the referential pronoun *that*. *Education* and *most students* are not parallel items.

Example H:

The reason he made a million dollars was because he had uncommon luck with the stock exchange.

Correction:

the *reason* ⎫ he made a million dollars
         ⎬ was
    that ⎭ he had uncommon luck with the stock exchange.

Note: The noun *reason* in this balanced structure must be paralleled by the *that . . .* noun clause, not by the conjunction *because* which introduces an adverbial clause.

Example I:

Just because he uses elegant expressions is no reason for your marrying him.

Correction:

The *fact* ⎫ that he uses elegant expressions
       ⎬ is no
  reason ⎭ for your marrying him.

Note: Again the balanced structure requires the noun *reason* to be matched with a parallel noun *fact,* not the conjunction *because* and an adverbial clause.

Note again: The sentence reads much better if put this way—*You should not marry him simply because he uses elegant expressions.* The fact that is horrible although not always easily avoidable.

EXERCISE XIII

In the sentences below identify the parallel ideas that should be stated in parallel structure. Rewrite the sentences.

1. The sentence was neither just nor according to proper legal procedure.

2. What we think of violence today betrays our philosophy, ethics, and the way we look at our fellow human beings.

3. An arbitrer of current fashion informs us that certain styles will come and go and come again but to maintain our sense of humor and good taste.

4. A tailback's publicity is often greater than a defense tackle.

5. Margaret was alert, superbly coordinated and with a delicate awareness of life's incongruities.

6. To advance theories and mentioning facts are two entirely different things.

7. United States, Russia, and the British are often friendly, although in many ways different in policy.

8. Sergeant Fuller decided to check the suspects' finger prints, get him a blood test, and to grant him his legal right to one telephone call.

9. Stephanie is a coed with exemplary manners and who therefore should be respected by all discerning collegians.

10. The reason for his impetuous action, as he explained it to Judge Malloy, was because he had a migraine headache.

11. In the detective's search of the premises he found several fingerprints, a snuffed-out cigarette, two unanswered letters and that the suspect was definitely Scandinavian.

12. The plays of Tennessee Williams, unlike Eugene O'Neil, do not have a gloomy, sombre atmosphere.

13. Marilyn is fascinating not only because she dresses in the best of latest fashion, but also with a commendable appropriateness.

14. Either we must acknowledge the growth of electronics and mass communication within the past two decades or be forever banished to an academic limbo.

15. Boswell praises Johnson's conduct and philosophy of life and that he was a down-to-earth practical man.

16. The Rotarians met in Atlantic City on Monday and Tuesday, and on Wednesday they left for their homes.

17. Not only were his ambitions unbridled and dangerous but also notoriously unpredictable.

18. Historians admonish us to remember our part, to take heed of its lessons, and being informed citizens of our present.

19. TWA makes travelling much more convenient and comfortable than cars.

20. Mark Twain was witty, sometimes caustic, often ambiguous and with a great awareness of the irony of life.

Subordination

PRINCIPLE

Less important ideas should always be subordinated to more important ones.

In the last few pages, on parallelism, we were dealing with ideas that were equal and therefore demanded coordination. Now our concern is a contrast: subordination.

Example:

Here are ideas as they may have originally presented themselves to the mind of Lewis Mumford.

A. This injury happened in the past.
   It happened when primitive man's powers, like ours today, had suddenly expanded.
   It was due essentially to an aberration, or a series of aberrations.
   these aberrations put man's most beneficent inventions at the command of his neurotic anxieties.

   Mumford organized his sentence by recognizing major and minor ideas.

B. This injury happened at a moment when primitive man's powers, like ours today, had suddenly expanded; and it was due essentially to an aberration, or a series of aberrations, which put his beneficent inventions at the command of his neurotic anxieties.

In order to subordinate properly, one has to be able to recognize the relationship of ideas. For instance, in this series of ideas

   it was raining
   he opened the umbrella
   he was walking down the street

It is necessary to see a causal (cause and effect, action and result) relationship between the first two ideas and a temporal (time) relationship between the first two and the third. The finished sentence could be this:

   Because it was raining as he was walking down the street, he opened the umbrella.

subordination—exercise

There are three ways of subordinating one idea to another:

1. by a dependent clause: He bought a Porsche which was made in Europe.
2. by a phrase: He bought a Porsche, made in Europe.
3. by a word: He bought a European Porsche.

Example:
The age of technology now surrounds us.
It boasts of its triumphs over nature.
One thing is ever more apparent to the anthropologist, or the student of man.

Revision:
In the age of technology which now surrounds us, and which boasts of its triumphs over nature, one thing is ever more apparent to the anthropologist—the student of man.
(Loren Eiseley)

Example:
We shared the same table.
Jean sat in the shade.
I was able to enjoy the sunlight.

Revision:
Although we shared the same table, Jean sat in the shade, whereas I was able to enjoy the sunlight.
(William Sansom)

Example:
She stood in front of the cabin fireplace.
She bent over.
She shook her head crossly.
Her hair was wet and yellow.
She was like a cat reproaching itself for not knowing better.
Her legs were wide apart.

Revision:
She stood in front of the cabin fireplace, her legs wide apart, bending over, shaking her wet yellow hair crossly, like a cat reproaching itself for not knowing better.
(Eudora Welty)

Example:
Mr. Dooley was a commercial traveller.
He had two sons in the Dominicans.
He also had a car of his own.
Socially he was miles ahead of us.
He had no false pride.

Revision:
Mr. Dooley was a commercial traveller with two sons in the Dominicans and a car of his own, so socially he was miles ahead of us, but he had not false pride.
(Frank O'Connor)

EXERCISE XIV

By subordinating as much as possible, combine each of the following groups of ideas into one sentence. (All these ideas originally appeared within the framework of one sentence.) State what you believe to be the main idea in the independent clause.

1. In the last generation critics have fought the battle for Ibsen.
   They have attempted to free him of the label of Social Problem playwright.
   They have tried to reveal him as a Faustian poet.
   For Ibsen social problems are only the visible data of a larger struggle.

2. On a certain night in 1923 Lawrence Tibbet made his operatic debut.
   For the rest of the season he was to continue in minor roles.
   He had not yet had time to learn major ones.

3. She is a fallen monument.
   She eventually shows herself to be susceptible to decay and death.
   She has ever held herself above the new order.
   She is unwilling to cope with it.
   Finally she dies.
   She is a symbol of a degenerating culture.
   Miss Emily is the central character in "A Rose for Emily."

4. In Victorian England the obstructionists were busy insulting Whitman and Swinburne.
   Whitman was one of the greatest poets in America.
   Swinburne was one of the greatest in England.
   Their techniques were different.
   Today both are accepted as writers of fine poetry.

5. Music gives pleasure.
   This pleasure may seem a rather elementary subject for discussion.
   The source of that pleasure is our musical instinct.
   This source is not at all elementary.
   It is, in fact, one of the prime puzzles of consciousness.

6. The contrast is striking today.
   We behold in one large part of the world a violently atheistic system.
   In the other part we see a secular culture.
   This culture may be neutral or friendly or hostile to religion.

7. There is a strong puritan bias in our national origin.
   This bias is mistrustful of emotional responses.
   It has also influenced education.
   Impulses, consequently, have been inhibited.
   Also the artistic imagination cannot take wing.

8. The humanities are a form of knowledge.
   It deals with man's life in nature and society.
   It is acquired through the study of man's spiritual creations.
   These creations are language, art, history, philosophy.

9. Thomas Blott spent many years on his back.
   After many years he was able to walk again.
   He had courage and determination to work again.

10. Everybody must give something for this cause.
    This is a cause that will benefit everybody.
    No sacrifice is too great.
    Nor is any too small.
    This is not a question of a luxury for one individual.

11. In today's world the needs of less fortunate people are not just next door.
    They are farflung and enormously complex.
    Charity organizations are an ever-present necessity.

12. At first glance the organs of the U.N. might appear to be comparable to those established in the U.S. Constitution.
    They are a senate, a house of representatives, a presidency.
    The U.N. also has an Economic and Social Council.
    This Council was championed by Senator Vandenberg.
    This was thrown in for good measure.

13. Some stars are hardly bigger than the earth.
    The majority are so large that hundreds of thousands of earths could be packed inside each.
    A few stars are so large that each can contain millions of millions of earths.
    The total number of stars in the universe is probably something like the total number of grains of sand on all the seashores of the world.

14. Sir Thomas More was ordered to sanction the king's divorce from Catherine of Aragon.
    The king wished this because he wanted to wed Anne Boleyn.
    More remained loyal to the Church of Rome.
    He refused to grant that a king can flout God's laws.
    Even a mighty king cannot do so.

15. This painting is the work of C. S. Raleigh.
    He is believed to be from Massachusetts.
    He painted in the 1880s.
    It shows a laughing polar bear.
    He is watching sailors in the longboats chase a whale through the waves.
    In the meanwhile tall ships stand by.

Emphatic and Effective Sentences

PRINCIPLE ONE

Put important words of a sentence in emphatic places—that is, at the beginning and end.

---

weak: However, George was weak.
strong: George, however, was weak.

weak: After all, malaria is no longer a dreaded disease at this time.
strong: Malaria, after all, is no longer a dreaded disease.

weak: Also the lyrics are stimulating, imaginative.
strong: The lyrics are stimulating, imaginative.

weak: There are three movies that serve to prove that there is still creativity in Hollywood.
strong: Three movies show the creativity of Hollywood.

weak: As a matter of fact, he is sick in bed at home.
strong: He is home sick in bed.

weak: Due to the fact that he is unreliable . . .
strong: Because he is unreliable . . .

PRINCIPLE TWO

On occasion sentences can be made more effective by placing certain words out of their normal position.

---

normal: The evil of a day is sufficient for that day.
stronger: Sufficient for the day is the evil thereof.

normal: The name for a woman is fickle.
stronger: Fickle, thy name is woman.

normal: I shall never admit impediments to the marriage of true minds.
stronger: Let me not to the marriage of true minds / Admit impediments.

normal: The home stands at the foot of the hill, in a grove of hemlock trees, and near the botanical gardens.

stronger: At the foot of the hill, in a grove of hemlock trees, and near the botanical gardens stands the home.

PRINCIPLE THREE

Active voice, as a rule, is more effective than passive voice.

---

dead: The rostrum was taken by the doughty old warrior, Randolph.

alive: The doughty old warrior, Randolph, took the rostrum.

dead: A contract to supply the Russians with machinery had to be signed by the Czechs before iron ore could be gotten.

alive: To obtain Russian iron ore, the Czechs had to sign a contract to supply the Russians with machinery.

dead: Some headway has already been made by the campaigner.

alive: The campaigner has already made some headway.

Note: In certain instances passive voice is more appropriate than the active. This is particularly true in more technical writing where the writer wishes to avoid any personal touch that may destroy the appearance of objectivity. For this reason, too, you will notice that practice varies among magazines. Popular magazines (*Time, Newsweek, The New Republic*) will use the active voice at least nine out of ten times. Trade magazines, science journals, and legal documents may have more passive than active. Even in the creative and popular writing an occasional passive voice is more effective than the active.

Examples.

The case was closed. There was nothing more to say.

He was thoroughly discouraged. For too many days he had been subjected to this cruel, relentless brainwashing.

PRINCIPLE FOUR

Try to arrange items in a series so that the most emphatic or important item comes at the end.

Examples:

> He was cheap, mean, utterly contemptible.
>
> She was a beauty, a charmer, a sheer phantom of delight.
>
> Thus was I sleeping by a brother's hand
> Of life, of crown, of queen at once dispatched.   (Hamlet)

Note: Familiarity with this method of emphasis can be helpful in literary criticism. In the last example, Hamlet, Sr., laments the sorrowful results of his death in order of ascending importance. By a brother's hand, he says, he was robbed of

- a) life (important, of course, but in a way the least important of the three results)
- b) crown (more important, because as king of Denmark he had a strong social-political responsibility)
- c) queen (most important, because she was his dearest possession. To be deprived of her and her love was worse than to be deprived of either life or kingship.)

EXERCISE XV

Revise each of the sentences below. In each case be able to explain why you believe the revised sentence is more emphatic or effective than the original.

1. The problem is: should man continue or cease to live.

2. Jacob's failure to report to the Board of Trustees was interpreted as due to the fact that he had no rational explanation for his behavior.

3. At the end of the protest, seven students had been seriously injured, it was reported in *The New York Times*.

4. Tom Flick was rescued from the fire by fireman Joe Stork who was pleased because he had been revealed as most adept at climbing stairs.

5. There are serious problems in the ghetto today waiting to be solved.

6. Some things in life are highly regarded by men: a good wife, normal children, economic security, and a Coke at midnight.

7. His motivation for violence and anger was that his wife was pregnant, anemic, and short of stature.

8. It is a generally accepted axiom that the spoils of war will be granted to the victor, the decision will be in favor of the opportunist, the praise will be garnered by the most deserving.

9. Joseph Murphy wasted his time, his talent, and two dollars at the race track.

10. After the dishes were finished, after the children were dressed for bed, and after the sun was down, the game was enjoyed by father on the television that was turned on.

11. Two errors in judgment could be found by Sherlock after a careful examination was made by him.

12. It was his open-mindedness that impressed the Dean when the prospective teacher was interviewed.

13. When I was waiting to check my baggage at Newark Airport, I ran into Paul Newman, of all things.

14. *Love Story* was read by millions of people as soon as it was published.

15. The academic changes will be explained by the advisors who will be met by the students in early April.

16. Frankenstein's monster turns out to be a rather sentimental creature at the end of the novel and film.

17. Jerry's last escapade with Charlotte will always be remembered by him.

18. Certainly, I shall not defend this criminal, in all probability.

19. This situation, so it seems to me, calls for serious attention, and, I say this in all sincerity, I intend to give it that kind of attention.

20. No unnecessary words should be used in a sentence.

PRINCIPLE FIVE

Avoid illogical constructions.

Examples (cf. examples *H and I,* under parallelism, pages 62–63):

1. *wrong:* The reason he failed was because he was sick.
   correct: The reason he failed was that he was sick.
   better: He failed because he was sick.

2. *wrong:* Because ancient Rome was corrupt caused its decline.
   correct: Corruption in ancient Rome caused its decline.

3. *confused:* One must wade through the school of hard knocks before arriving at success.

   explanation: The triteness of metaphor results in confusion. Does one wade through a school of hard knocks? Really?

4. *confused:* He floated down the feathery bed of ease and meandered over the primrose path of dalliance.
   correct: He was a no-good playboy.

   explanation: Again trite metaphors should be eliminated for clarity and economy.

5. *wrong:* A blizzard is when you have a violent windstorm with driving snow and intense cold.
   correct: A blizzard is violent windstorm with driving snow and intense cold.

   explanation: The adverbial *when*-clause cannot be set up as an equivalent to the noun *blizzard*.

6. *wrong:* A touchdown is where one crosses the goal line with the football.
   correct. A player scores a touchdown when he crosses the goal line.

   explanation: The adverbial clause (*where one crosses . . .*) cannot function in this way.

PRINCIPLE SIX

Important relationships and subordinations must be made obvious in the sentence structure; they should not be left unrelated in compound sentences.

---

unrelated: Mr. Bell is a tax collector and he is sixty years old.
related: Mr. Bell, a tax collector, is sixty years old.
subordinate: Mr. Bell, who is sixty years old, is a tax collector.

unrelated: It was nine o'clock and he decided to leave.
related: At nine o'clock he decided to leave.
subordinate: Since it was nine o'clock, he decided to leave.

unrelated: Vice President Agnew steered clear of his criticism of broadcasting practice and he chose instead to analyze the electronic media in broad terms.

better: In his analysis of the electronic media, Vice President Agnew steered clear of his criticisms of broadcasting practices.

unrelated: Barbra Streisand is a fine actress and she has a strong voice.

better: Barbra Streisand, who has a strong voice, is also a fine actress.

Note: In normal conversation it would be absurd to expect this kind of subordination. After a telephone conversation Barb says to Steve: "That was Anne on the phone. She is feeling rather low. She is coming over to see us." Steve would react rather coldly if she said: "Anne, who just called and who is feeling low, is coming over to see us."

A FINAL WORD ON SENTENCES

As much as possible, try to keep subject and predicate, predicate and object together.

Examples:

confusing: A paragraph, to be brief and not to waste time, is a series of sentences having unity and coherence.

better: Briefly, a paragraph is a series of sentences. . . .

awkward: At the Command Performance he sang, with a great deal of professional ease, the title song from *Oklahoma!*

better: At the Command Performance he sang the title song from *Oklahoma!* with a great deal of professional ease.

EXERCISE XVI

Improve the following sentences. Eliminate illogical constructions and show the relationship of all ideas.

1. One does not have to drill deep to tap his milk of human kindness.

2. To make an error is when the shortstop throws over the head of the first baseman.

3. The sociologist Murray is short-tempered and has a remarkable memory.

4. Because war cannot go on forever causes hope even in the most pessimistic person.

5. To make a decision is when a man will step forward to be heard because he believes he is right.

6. Myrna is, by the way, a provocative person, who is, if you will take my word for it, a dedicated student of art, so to speak.

7. To play a Chopin sonata in the proper way is after you have studied both Chopin and the art of the piano.

8. Massachusetts is an important state and it has a crucial position when it comes to presidential primaries.

THE PRONOUN

Antecedents and Pronouns

PRINCIPLE

A pronoun must agree with its antecedent in number. This antecedent (i.e., the noun or named concept to which the pronoun refers) must always be clear and definite.

Examples:

Many *Presidents* wrote *their* memoirs.	**antecedent and pronoun are plural**
President *Grant* wrote *his* memoirs at the urging of Twain.	**antecedent and pronoun are singular**

Note: A collective noun (*jury, herd, flock, army, committee, couple,* etc.), when taken as a unit, demands a singular pronoun; when the members of a group act separately or as individuals a plural pronoun is needed.

Examples:

The *jury* returned *its* verdict of not guilty.	**the jury acts as a unit**
After the *jury* took *their* seats, they discussed the case.	**each member takes a chair**
The *committee* submitted *its* report in the morning.	**committee acts as a unit**
The *committee* voiced *their* opinions before casting six favorable votes and three negative.	**members of committee act as individuals**

Note: the following indefinite pronouns are conventially considered singular:

each	anyone	someone
every	anybody	somebody
everyone	nobody	either
everybody		neither

None can be either singular or plural.

Because these singular pronouns are used in reference to individuals in a group, they are particularly vulnerable to "misuse" with plural pronouns in violation of conventional formal use. It requires conscious effort to overcome the irregular usage of informal speech. "Everybody has their day," may be all right in informal talk. Most grammarians prefer, "Everybody has his day."

Examples:

Each of the students *is* expected to do *his* work as well as *he* can.
I do not expect *either* of them to do better than *he* has done.
None of them *were* able to find *their* identification cards.
None of the jewelry *was* found, for the thief had taken everything.

Note:

A. *And* joins antecedents and makes them plural.
B. *Or* and *nor* separate antecedents and make them *singular,* when the antecedent after *or* and *nor* is singular.
C. *Or* and *nor* separate antecedents and make them *plural* when the antecedent after *or* and *nor* is plural.

Examples:

Singleton *and* Duelton have had *their* disagreements.
Neither John *nor* Peter *was* able to use *his* voice properly.
Either the spectators *or* the *umpire is* wrong in *his* viewpoint.
Either the umpire *or* the *spectators are* wrong in *their* viewpoint.

Note: A noun or pronoun preceding a gerund is in the possessive case (if the noun or pronoun is not itself a direct object of the verb).

Examples:

I was surprised at *his* coming so soon.
(Compare: I was surprised at *his* early arrival.)

He was annoyed at *John's* leaving before breakfast.
(Compare: He was annoyed at *John's* attitude.)

He could not understand *my* running down the corridor.
But: He could not see me running down the corridor.
(That is, he could not see *me* while I was running; *me* in this instance is the direct object of see.)

Note: Which is commonly used for non-restrictive clauses, *that* for restrictive, provided that the sentence permits this distinction.

Examples:

My Fair Lady, which was a great success, made Julie Andrews famous.
The musical play that made Julie Andrews famous was *My Fair Lady.*
But: It was that play which made Julie Andrews famous.

(The repetition of *that* would be awkward: "It was that play that made Julie Andrews famous.")

Note: The case of *whoever* (i.e., the choice between *whoever* and *whomever*) is determined by the relative clause and not by the main clause.

Examples:

We shall take *whoever* is outstanding in physics.
(Compare: We shall take him *who* is outstanding in physics.)

We shall take *whoever* you think is outstanding in physics.
(Do not be fooled by *you think*, which is not an integral part of the relative clause.)

We shall take *whomever* you find outstanding.
(*Whomever* is object of *find.*)

Note: Avoid these common difficulties:

A. *wrong:* It is between him and I.
  (*I* is the object of the preposition *between.*)
 right: It is between him and *me.*
 right: He and I know what is right.
  (*I* is the subject of the verb *know.*)
 right: It is *I.* (formal writing)
 right: It's *me.* (perfectly acceptable in colloquial and informal language)

B.   *wrong:* I am right, *aren't* I?
     right: I am right, *am* I *not?* (Stuffy, to be sure, but correct.) Am
             I *not* right?
             (Leave *aren't I* to the pretentious.)

EXERCISE XVII

Correct the following sentences wherever necessary.

1. Each juror should examine the evidence carefully before casting their vote.

2. The jury through its foreman announced the verdict, not-guilty.

3. Neither Notre Dame nor Oklahoma are expected to have an undefeated season.

4. Both Rick and Tony denied any guilt but everyone on the scene knew it was them who they saw commit the crime.

5. The mob of bedraggled men and confused women were shouting at their public enemy.

6. Every tennis player who earnestly tries can improve their game in time.

7. We have no idea whom you think will be the grand-prize winners.

8. Neither the children nor their fathers would accept the responsibility for their actions.

9. The uninformed spectator does not know who to trust in this nefarious matter.

10. No one could explain or understand Ray denying his influence in last week's political purge.

11. Apparently everybody except Lois and I saw the accident.

12. The next president will be whoever the majority of people vote for.

13. The baseball team, which is ahead on the Fourth of July, usually wins the pennant.

14. The lawyer remembered him saying that on the night of August 6 he never left his home.

15. The loss of the game was attributed to the shortstop making three errors.

STRANGE OR TROUBLESOME VERBS

Group *I:*   Lie = Lay*

	A. intransitive	B. transitive
past	lie (recline)	lay (place)
past	lay	laid
perfect	lain	laid

Group II: Sit = set

	A. intransitive	B. transitive
present	sit (be seated)	set (put in position)
past	sat	set
perfect	sat	set

Group III: Rise = raise

	A. intransitive	B. transitive
present	rise (get up)	raise (lift up)
past	rose	raised
perfect	risen	raised

Examples—Group I

A. We *lie* in the sand by day and in bed at night.
A. We are *lying* in the sun.
B. We *lay* the books on the table.
B. We are *laying* the books on the table.
} present

A. We *lay* in the sun for three hours yesterday.
B. We *laid* the books on the table.
} past

A. We *have lain* in the sun so long that we are burned.
B. We *have laid* countless books on the table.
} perfect

---

*If one says, "I'm going to lay down for an hour," the intention is perfectly clear even though some pedants may say that "I'm going to lie down for an hour" is proper. In order to placate these finicky people it might be prudent to use "lie down."

verbs—linking

Examples—Group II

A. We sit in semi-darkness cursing our lot in life.
A. We are sitting in semi-darkness.
B. We set the books on the shelf.
B. We are setting the books on the shelf.

} present

A. We *sat* on the bench all afternoon.
B. We *set* the books on the shelf yesterday.

} past

A. We *have sat* in one place all day.
B. We *have set* many books on the shelf during our lifetime.

} perfect

Examples—Group III

A. We *rise* from the table to toast the bride.
B. We *raise* the glasses in a toast.

} present

A. We *rose* at six o'clock yesterday.
B. We *raised* the glasses in a toast yesterday.

} past

A. We *have risen* at six o'clock for the past six weeks.
B. We *have* often *raised* the glasses in a toast.

} perfect

1. Note the forms of the following verbs. Those marked with asterisks are the forms most frequently misused.

present	past	perfect
bear	bore	* borne
burst	* burst	* burst
dive	dived or dove	* dived
drink	drank	* drunk
hang (suspend)	hung	hung
hang (execute)	hanged	hanged
lead	led	* led
pay	paid (not payed)	paid
shine	shone	shone
swim	swam	* swum
swing	swung	swung
wake	woke, waked	waked
wring	* wrung	wrung

2. After certain linking verb (*seems*, *becomes*) and verbs of the senses (*feel*, *look*, *smell*, *taste*, *sound*) we usually use adjectives, not adverbs.

Examples:

A. The candidate seems (appears) strong and healthy.
   He felt good after going to church.
   She appears confident.

B. Pearl looks pert and young. Susan looks sharp.
   (Contrast: Susan looks sharply at all pearls. *Sharply* describes the manner in which she observes.)

   Randall feels resentful but nonetheless grateful.
   Randall feels around the darkened room carefully.

   The mother's skin feels tender.
   She feels her child tenderly.

   Although the highball smelled strong, it tasted weak.

   After enduring so much contemporary music, a classicist turns to music that to him sounds good.

C. Melvin feels good because he feels well. (Note *well,* as used here, is an adjective, not an adverb.)

   So also: Because Oliver danced well last night, he feels good today. Psychologically, Joe is not well because he did not do well in his finals.

3. Observe the distinction between *leave* and *let.*

   Let the books stay where they are. (i.e., let them alone)
   Leave the books on the table. (i.e., deposit them on the table)

   wrong: Lois left me do the chores alone.
   right: Lois let me do the chores alone.
   right: After Lois left me, I had to do the chores alone.

EXERCISE XVIII

1. Stella (set, sat) the chair in front of the window so she could see all her relatives (setting, sitting) on the verandah.

2. Some salad dressings taste (sour, sourly) even though they look (sweet, sweetly).

3. His chances for re-employment (lie, lay) in the hands of his immediate supervisor.

4. She immediately (rose, raised) and left the table.

5. He (raised, rose) himself from the same table and (sat, set) beside her.

6. Hyacinths smell (clean, cleanly) in spring.

7. Tim was told to (leave, let) the trimmings in good shape by not (sitting, setting) them where they could be trampeled on.

8. Oscar recognized the task that (lay, laid) before him but did not turn back.

9. (Leave, let) the sherrif challenge the outlaws alone if he so insists.

10. The challenger looks (confident, confidently) into the opposite corner where the champion appears (nervous, nervously).

11. She (lay, laid) in bed with a headache all morning, longer than she had (lain, laid) there in all her life.

12. Congress sometimes (leaves, lets) the final decision up to the President.

13. The child was (laying, lying) in a crib much too small for her size.

14. His father was (setting, sitting) the gear in the boat by himself, because John continued to (lay, lie) on the cot.

15. He has (laid, lain) the responsibility on her once too often; now he must (lie, lay) in the bed of his own choice.

DICTION

Words and Expressions Frequently Misused

The following words or expressions in one way or another cause difficulty when used in formal or semiformal expository writing. Trite and colloquial expressions may be appropriate for informal speech (sometimes they are unavoidable), but in careful writing their use often indicates that the writer has no sense of style or appropriateness, or that he is completely unaware of the meaning he wishes to convey.

Absolutely
Wholly, completely; do not use as an intensive—e.g., "Ladies Absolutely Forbidden." They are either forbidden or not, and no "absolutely" about it. (*Ladies:* see below) Avoiding the use of "absolutely" is "absolutely" necessary.

No: "Jonas is absolutely absurd."
Yes: "This is absurd."

Affect, effect
Affect means to *influence; effect* (the verb) means *to bring about* as a result or fact.

e.g., Cloudly skies did not *affect* his cheerful disposition.
The doctor *effected* a complete cure. (His cure was an effect of the doctor's knowledge and care.)

Aggravate
To intensify, to make worse; in expository writing, do not use in sense of *to annoy, irritate, provoke.* Stay away from "aggravate." You don't need it.

e.g., The dirt *aggravated* the soreness of the wound. (right)
His pettiness *aggravated* me. (colloquial)

Agree to,
agree with
The first is used for things, the second for people.
e.g., All the delegates *agreed* to the proposal.
All the delegates *agreed with* the speaker.

Ain't
Although the latest edition of Merriam-Webster's Unabridged Dictionary lists this word, it is not proper usage in careful speaking or writing. Still, "Ain't" is

a respectable word except for the finicky. We can say "we aren't," "they weren't," "you aren't" but we can't say "I amn't." Why not say "I ain't"? Besides, the word has been in use for centuries; it is about time it gains due recognition.

Alibi

From Latin meaning "in another place"—therefore, the proof that one was elsewhere at the time of a crime. Do not use in the sense of an excuse.

e.g., The jury accepted his *alibi*.
What is your *alibi* for not stopping? (colloquial)

All the farther,
all the higher

Unacceptable substitute for *as far as, as high as*
e.g., This is *as far as* (not *all the farther*) I can go.

Allusion, illusion

Allusion is an indirect reference; *illusion* is a false impression or appearance.

e.g., The writer made an *allusion* to the play *Hamlet*.
Drowsy eyes are often misled by *illusions*.

Alright

There is no such word; use *all right*. Confusion comes by analogy with *already* (by that time) and all ready (altogether ready).

Anyplace

Use *anywhere*, especially in formal writing.

No: "I am not going anyplace tonight."
Yes: "I am not going anywhere tonight."

As, like

As is a conjunction, *like* a preposition.

e.g., He, *like* Churchill, agreed too quickly with Stalin.
Ice cream tastes good *as* ice cream should.

Back of,
in back of

Unacceptable substitutes for *behind*.

e.g., The church is *behind* (not *in back of*) the school.

Beside, besides

Beside means *at the side of; besides* is both preposition and adverb meaning *in addition to*.

e.g., He sat *beside* her in the wilderness.
Besides, a loaf of bread is not enough.
Besides the bread, he brought a jug of wine.

Between, among

Between is used for two, or to indicate reciprocal relations when there are more than two; *among* is used for three or more.

e.g., The fight was *between* Muhammed Ali and Frazier.

A treaty *between* each of the five nations . . . .
There was not a murmur *among* all the opponents.

Blame on	At best colloquial for *blame*. e.g., He blamed Nixon for the mistake. Do not say, "He blamed the mistake on Nixon." Can a person really blame a mistake?
But that, but what	Do not use these with the verb *to doubt;* leave *but that, but what* with sports announcers. e.g., We do not *doubt* that they will win.
Can, may	It is not old-fashioned to say "May I go?" when asking permission, and "Can I go?" when in doubt about your ability.
Compare to	Used to point out similarities between objects that are of a different order or species. e.g., The easy life is often compared to a bed of roses. "Shall I compare thee to a summer's day?" St. Paul compares life to a battle.
Compare with	Points out differences and similarities between objects that are of the same order or species. e.g., Compare Pittsburgh with Cleveland. He compared the translation with the original.
Complected	Not a formally acceptable substitution for correct but awkward *complexioned*. e.g., Hilda is light complexioned. Better: "Hilda has a light complexion."
Credible, credulous	*Credible*—able to be believed, believable; *credulous*—ready or disposed to believe, especially on slight evidence. e.g., The story of his childhood is *credible*. Your braggadocio has made him *credulous*.
Different from	Do not substitute *different than*, although *different than* seems to be gaining in popularity. e.g., She is greatly *different from* her sister in looks.
Differ from, differ with	*Differ from* stresses unlikeness; *differ with* stresses disagreement.

e.g., An Englishman *differs* from a Frenchman.
Russians *differ* with Americans on many issues.

Due to,
because of

Due to is an adjective; *because of* is an adverb—but most grammarians tolerate *due to* as an adverb.

e.g., His irritability was *due* to a severe headache.
Because of the tense international situation, many tourists stayed away from China.

Each other,
one another

Each other is used with two objects or persons; *one another* with more than two. This distinction is rapidly breaking down.

e.g., Husband and wife help *each other* in many ways.
Students must treat *one another* with respect.

Enormity,
enormousness

Enormity designates something monstrously wicked or criminal; *enormousness* designates bigness.

e.g., The bystanders were shocked at the *enormity* of his crime.
Spectators are thrilled by the *enormousness* of Hoover Dam.

Enthuse

Above all, do not become enthusiastic about this scrawny word.

Etc.

A Latin abbreviation for *and the rest;* therefore, it is redundant to write *and etc.* In general, avoid its use in expository writing. Excessive use of *etc.* is a sure sign of sloppy thinking.

Guess

In formal speech and writing, do not use in the sense of *think, believe.*

e.g., I *believe* (not guess) he is right.

Irregardless

There is no such word in formal English; use *regardless. Irregardless* enters by way of confusion with *irrespective (respective).*

Lady

The proper femine counterpart of gentleman. Do not use as a substitute for *woman.* Of course, most Americans would like to think all women are ladies, but we should be somewhat skeptical.

e.g., A woman (not a *lady*) comes in to do the laundry.
She wore her clothes like a *lady.*
The women (not *ladies*) are playing cards.

diction

Liable, likely	*Liable* suggests something undesirable; *likely* suggests probability.
	e.g., If you go through a red light, you are *liable* to a fine; and if a policeman sees you, you are *likely* to receive one.
Nice	Overused, meaningless—avoid except in sense of *precise*.
	No: "She is a nice girl."
	Yes: "The scientist made a nice distinction."
Off of	The preposition is *off*.
	e.g., He fell off (not off of) the ladder.
On account of	A strange but colloquial way of expressing *because*.
	e.g., I could not come because (not *on account of*) I sprained my ankle.
Plan on	Colloquial usage with participle; use *plan to* with verb.
	e.g., I *plan to* take a trip. (not *plan on taking*)
Quite a few	Avoid in formal writing—a colloquial expression
	e.g., We expected a large number at the dance. (not *quite a few*)
Someplace	Colloquial for *somewhere*.
Take in	Colloquial for *to attend*.
	e.g., I shall attend (not take in) a lecture.
These kind	Illiterate for *this kind*. In sense, "these kind" is correct; in grammar, it is unacceptable.
Treat with	No proper substitute for *treat of*.
	e.g., The paper treats of (not treats with) many debatable principles.
Uninterested, disinterested	*Uninterested* pertains to lack of interest; *disinterested* designates impartiality.
	e.g., He is totally uninterested in amoebas.
	A good umpire is always disinterested.
Unique	Means *without a like, but one*.
	e.g., The conspiracy was unique (not *the most unique in history. Most unique* is much worse than a

double superlative because it betrays ignorance of the basic meaning of *unique*.

Would, should   Both can express a conditional future; *should* can be used for the first person; *would* must be used for the second and third person. This distinction is rapidly breaking down.

e.g., I (we) should be happy to interview you if you are in the vicinity.

or   I (we) would be happy to interview you if . . .
You would be happy to see me if . . .
He (they) would be happy to see me if . . .

Note: The condition need not be explicitly stated.

Would   Also can express:
(1) a conditional willingness,

e.g., We would finish the work if you allowed us.

(2) customary action in the past.

e.g., We would go on a family picnic every Fourth.

Should   Can express obligation.

e.g., You should be punctual.

INTRODUCTION

This *Handbook* presumes that the paragraph, and not the sentence, is the basic unit of thought and communication. The statement may seem to be a dogmatic assertion without proof or logic; but after close analysis one finds that we do, ordinarily, think and speak in paragraph form. Thus, even the simple sentence: "It is a fine day," is implicitly at least a paragraph. Why is the speaker able to make such a statement in the first place? His process of thought could be along these lines: "I had a good night's rest. I have plenty to eat and to drink and enough money. I am in good health. The sun is shining. I made an A in history this morning. Finally, I have a date with my favorite girl tonight. Therefore, *it is a fine day.*"

The sentence about the nature of the day, then, is an embryo paragraph; or we might say it is a topic sentence begging for development. Consider the first paragraph again. The statement about the basic unit of communication also had to be developed if the reader's acceptance is wanted. All ideas cry out for development or proof. It is possible, then, to define a paragraph as *an idea with development or proof.*

To be able to write a paragraph, as stated in the *Preface,* does not mean that one can write a full-length book, an essay, or even a short article. It simply means that one can state an idea and develop it with a certain amount of coherence. The ability to write a paragraph is a literary asset. To tie paragraphs together, make an idea flow from a preceding one and lead into another is a talent that must be worked at to be realized.

Proof

Proof is a strong word in this context, but it is entirely appropriate. Even in our prosaic, everyday conversation we do not simply make statements or voice opinions (unless we are talking to morons or the incredibly guillible) without proceeding to prove why these statements or opinions are acceptable. Most people will not accept the following statements without some kind of protest: "My fiancée is the most beautiful girl in the world," and "The Steelers are the greatest team in football." The first statement calls for a definition of beauty and a description of the girl. Even then it is questionable whether the statement will be accepted without demur. For the repudiation of the second statement all one must do is refer to the records, which in this case should be convincing. In both cases, however, proof, one way or the other, is necessary.

Methods of Development

There are various ways of proving or developing an idea. We can

1. define or describe it
2. submit examples or illustrations of it
3. compare it, contrast it, give an analogy of it
4. give reasons for it, or put it through the process of induction and deduction
5. set the idea in time, in space, or in narrative form.

These are the principal means of development, but they must not be thought of as the only or exclusive means. In practice, most paragraphs are the result of a combination of several ways of development.

Unity

While developing ideas, we must keep a keen eye on two things: unity and coherence. Unity in paragraphing means that all parts of the paragraph are related to the topic sentence or central idea. Nothing irrelevant can be tolerated unless it is distinctly understood that what is inserted is irrelevant, an aside. The unity of a paragraph developing the idea of a fine day would be shattered if we inserted a statement about the length of Charlemagne's beard. So also, if we are talking about the pleasure of walking, we cannot turn to a discussion of the price of a tuba in Cuba. It is important to check each paragraph to see whether all details, all parts relate clearly and logically to the topic sentence.

Coherence

Everybody must strive for coherence, something that is brought about by proper transitions and clear order. Coherence demands that everything belongs together and, by transitional means, clearly is together. Unity and coherence are like the brick and mortar of a building. For one thing, unity of a building presupposes that we have the right kind and number of bricks, that they fit together. For another, coherence presumes not only that the bricks be piled one on another, but also that they hold fast. So also in paragraphs the material must relate to the topic sentence and join together in such a way that the reader will be able to see the relationship of each part.

Transitions

There are many ways of making transitions in order to show coherence. In the following examples, the italicized words suggest some of these ways; note that it is possible to follow the line of thought by these means of transition, even though most of the sentences are not completed.

A. There are three ways of making life interesting. *First,* one can devote . . . *Second,* he can choose to . . . *Third,* he might try to save . . . *But* these ways are not exclusive, *for* we can find . . . *Therefore,* it is best to proceed cautiously.

B. It is almost the definition of a gentleman to say that . . . *This definition* is . . .

C. Martha is not one to be offended easily. *She* does, *however,* resent . . . *When* she first awakens, *she* . . . *Then* Martha is apt to be under a strain . . . *Soon afterwards,* she will take on a different attitude. *This attitude* is reflected in her disposition toward . . . *Since she* would be the first to admit this psychological quirk, one need not . . . *All in all, she* impresses one with *her* . . .

D. I apologize to Professor Smith for *this* statement. May I point out, *nevertheless,* that he . . . *Furthermore,* where would he be if I had not made *this statement? In one way,* it should not have been taken seriously. *In another,* it should have been . . . *My apology, then,* must be accepted in *this* light.

The following paragraph is a partially reduced paragraph from Nathaniel Hawthorne ("The Artist of the Beautiful," 1844). Most of the transitional material has been deleted. Even though the paragraph in this adapted form has unity, it does not have coherence.

Her father withdrew his finger. The butterfly appeared to recover the power of voluntary motion, while its hues assumed much of their original lustre. When transferred from Danforth's hand, this radiance grew so powerful that it positively threw the little fellow's shadow back against the wall. He extended his plump hand and watched the waving of the insect's wings with infantile delight. There was a certain odd expression of sagacity on his face.

Below is the same paragraph, but now the transitional material has been added. Almost immediately, we notice how important they are for the sense of the paragraph.

Her father withdrew his finger. The butterfly *then* appeared to recover the power of voluntary motion, while its hues assumed much of their original lustre. *At first,* when transferred from Danforth's hand, this radiance grew so powerful that it positively threw the little fellow's shadow back against the wall. He, *meanwhile,* extended his plump hand and watched the waving of the insect's wings with infantile delight. *Nevertheless,* there was a certain odd expression of sagacity on his face.

Appropriate transitions are essential to good composition. The repetition of key words, the use of pronouns, the use of synonyms, and the careful arrangement of grammatical structure all help to make these transitions clear.

Transitional Words and Phrases

A writer should appreciate the usefulness of such words as these:

1. for example, for instance, in this way, namely
2. but, however, still, nevertheless, on the other hand, to the contrary, either-or, neither-nor
3. when, after, before, beforehand, afterward, immediately, then, now, soon, thereafter, later, earlier
4. and, also, too, furthermore, moreover, secondly, thirdly, in addition to, in this manner, in like manner
5. therefore, finally, as a consequence, as a result, accordingly.

Length of Paragraphs

The length of paragraphs varies greatly. In the eighteenth and nineteenth centuries it was customary to write paragraphs from 600 to 1,000 or more words in length. Today the tendency is to write shorter ones, averaging between 200 and 300 words, but with extremes of one word and 1,000 words.

There are two important suggestions to keep in mind. First, remember that the original purpose of sectioning off parts of an article into paragraphs was for the sake of the eye. Notice, for instance, how much easier it is to begin reading a page with four or five indentations than a page with only one or none. Secondly, know for whom and for what you are writing. A paper written for children ordinarily will have shorter paragraphs than one written for adults. One written for amusement will not equal the length of paragraphs of another written for a solemn occasion. *Time Magazine* or *Newsweek* will not print the long paragraphs of PMLA or any scientific and technical journal.

NEWMAN'S DEFINITION OF A GENTLEMAN

The following is approximately one-half of one paragraph written by John Henry Newman in the nineteenth century. If he were living today and writing for *Time Magazine,* he might very well begin to write it in this fashion. Upon careful reading one notices how the whole material does have paragraph unity and does develop the topic sentence. But one also notices that it lends itself well to subdivisions that can be considered separate paragraph entities in themselves.

Pain and the Gentleman. It is almost a definition of a gentleman to say he is one who never inflicts pain. This description is both refined and, as far as it goes, accurate. He is mainly occupied in merely removing the obstacles which hinder the free and unembarrassed action of those about him; and he concurs with their movements rather than takes the initiative himself.

An Easy Chair and a Good Fire. His benefits may be considered as parallel to what are called comforts or conveniences in arrangements of a personal nature: like an easy chair or a good fire, which do their part in dispelling cold and fatigue, though nature provides both means of rest and animal heat without them. The true gentleman in like manner carefully avoids whatever may cause a jar or a jolt in the minds of those with whom he is cast;—all clashing of opinion, or collision of feeling, all restraint, or suspicion, or gloom, or resentment; his great concern being to make every one at their ease and at home.

He has his eyes on all his company; he is tender towards the bashful, gentle towards the distant, and merciful towards the absurd; he can recollect to whom he is speaking; he guards against unseasonable illusions, or topics which may irritate; he is seldom prominent in conversation, and never wearisome.

Heroic Self-effacement. He makes light of favors while he does them, and seems to be receiving when he is conferring. He never speaks of himself except when compelled, never defends himself by a mere retort, he has no ears for slander or gossip, is scrupulous in imputing motives to those who interfere with him and interprets everything for the best.

He is never mean or little in his disputes, never takes unfair advantage, never mistakes personalities or sharp sayings for arguments, or insinuates evil which he dare not say out. From a long-sighted prudence, he observes the maxim of the ancient sage, that we should ever conduct ourselves towards our enemy as if he were one day to be our friend.

With Malice Toward None. He has too much good sense to be affronted at insults, he is too well employed to remember injuries, and too indolent to bear malice. He is patient, forbearing and resigned on philosophical principles . . .

THE PARAGRAPH OF DEFINITION AND DESCRIPTION

Introduction

The way one develops an idea depends in large measure upon the purpose of the writer and the nature of the idea. If, for instance, Pete wishes to explain to Dan that he had a happy time last night at the dance, he will most likely go into a description of the evening, noting such details as the style of the band, the quality and quantity of the food, the sights and smells of the dance floor, the liveliness of his dancing partner, and so forth. At the end of his description, if he is in any way effective, he should have his friend convinced that the evening was an enjoyable one.

An important point must be made here. When you set out to describe a person or an event, you should not rely solely or mainly on evaluative adjectives. Such statements as "She is a beautiful girl," "It was a tremendous ball game" are ineffective because they make a judgment without proof. Instead, if you say Joni Garrison has this kind of figure and describe the color of her eyes and complexion, her height, her weight, the texture of her hair and so on, then your reader or listener can form his own opinion. If you are extraordinarily effective, you not only convince, you re-create.

To define means to set limits or boundaries. Thus, if one is to define man, he must set up the limits within which he can exist and beyond which he cannot. One can set the first limit by saying man is an animal. If he adds that man has the gift of reason, he makes an even greater discrimination. Definition, therefore, works by inclusion and exclusion, stating what a thing is and what it is not.

Let us suppose that, after one has finished defining what a man is, he wishes to continue by determining what or who a *particular* man is—let us say, Joel Rich. The tendency now will be to veer away from definition strictly speaking and turn toward description. Description, more than definition, works by addition, supplying detail and telling us what a thing is or does. Thus, description will tell us that Joel Rich is blond, 6'2", 180 pounds, blue-eyed, long-nosed, thin-lipped, freckled; that he works for General Motors, plays golf four times a week, attends church three times a week, and gives generously to the Red Cross.

In practice, and in so far as non-technical writing is concerned, there is little distinction between definition and description. If a writer's purpose is identification, he will no doubt rely on both methods; in other words, he will both include and exclude. The following diagrams illustrate the technique of this kind of paragraphing.

Topic: We shall now define man.

Development:

What man is NOT

What man IS

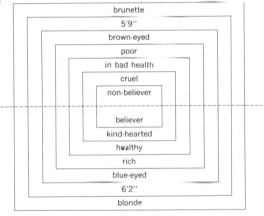

```
┌─────────────────────────────┐
│         non-existent        │
│ ┌─────────────────────────┐ │
│ │        non-living       │ │
│ │ ┌─────────────────────┐ │ │
│ │ │      vegetable      │ │ │
│ │ │ ┌─────────────────┐ │ │ │
│ │ │ │   non-rational  │ │ │ │
│ │ │ │                 │ │ │ │
│ │ │ │     rational    │ │ │ │
│ │ │ └─────────────────┘ │ │ │
│ │ │       animal        │ │ │
│ │ └─────────────────────┘ │ │
│ │         living          │ │
│ └─────────────────────────┘ │
│          existent           │
└─────────────────────────────┘
```

Topic: We shall now describe Joel Rich.

Development:

What Joel Rich is NOT

What Joel Rich IS

```
brunette
5'9"
brown-eyed
poor
in bad health
cruel
non-believer

believer
kind-hearted
healthy
rich
blue-eyed
6'2"
blonde
```

I

(1) Historians state that *some* colonial settlements hanged witches, while *other* communities "ducked" them. (2) *To the average reader*, this seems like surprisingly unequal punishment—but only because he fails to understand the true nature of the "ducking" a witch received. (3) *In our culture* the word ducking tends to have pleasant associations: it suggests bobbing for apples or horseplay at the old swim-

coherence by cataloging

what ducking means to various groups—note transitional words beginning sentences

sentences 2–5: what ducking is NOT

ming hole. (4) *Or,* if the reader has dipped lightly into history, he may have encountered the ancient practice of strapping shrewish women to seats resembling closestools and then plunging them briefly into water. (5) *Once again,* the connotations are comic rather than formidable. (6) *Actually, however,* the ducking of witches was far from being mere harmless slapstick. A woman accused of witchcraft was *first* stripped naked, and often beaten; *then* she was bound tightly, hand and foot; *finally,* she was cast into the water. (7) *If she floated,* that fact automatically proved her guilt; she was hauled ashore and promptly hanged. (8) *If she sank,* she was without supernatural powers and therefore presumably innocent—*but,* unfortunately, she was also usually dead from drowning and therefore unable to enjoy her vindication. (9) *One witch,* indeed, almost beat the game. (10) *When ducked,* she floated and thus did not drown; *when hanged,* she somehow escaped suffocation or a broken neck and was cut down alive. (11) *But* the town fathers were resourceful; they bound her again, stretched her out on the ground and piled heavy stones on her until she was "pressed" to death. (12) Justice, it seems, was not to be denied.*

contrast—transition to what it IS

sequence of time— description of what it is

two alternatives—note balance of sentences

contrast

developed by example note balanced sentence 10—transition by time

transitional word—contrast

Note variety of sentences indicated in one way by their size.

Sentence 1	—	13 words
Sentence 2	—	26 words
Sentence 5	—	9 words
Sentence 11	—	28 words
Last sentence	—	7 words

With sentence 9 Jones turns from description to example. As mentioned before, seldom do we have a paragraph developed in only one way.

*Alexander E. Jones, from *Creative Exposition,* copyright 1957 by Holt, Rinehart and Winston, Inc. Reprinted by permission of the publisher.

II

(1) Stephen closed his eyes and held out in the air his trembling hand with the palm upwards. (2) He felt the prefect of studies touch it for a moment at the fingers to straighten it and then the swish of the sleeve of the soutane as the pandybat was lifted to strike. (3) A hot burning stinging tingling blow like the loud crack of a broken stick made his trembling hand crumple together like a leaf in the fire: and at the sound and the pain scalding tears were driven into his eyes. (4) His whole body was shaking with fright, his arm was shaking and his crumpled burning livid hand shook like a loose leaf in the air. (5) A cry sprang to his lips, a prayer to be let off. (6) But though the tears scalded his eyes and his limbs quivered with pain and fright he held back the hot tears and the cry that scalded his throat.

(7) —Other hand! shouted the prefect of studies.

(8) Stephen drew back his maimed and quivering right arm and held out his left hand. (9) The soutane sleeve swished again as the pandybat was lifted and a loud crashing sound and a fierce maddening tingling burning pain made his hand shrink together with the palms and fingers in a livid quivering mass. (10) The scalding water burst forth from his eyes and, burning with shame and agony and fear, he drew back his shaking arm in terror and burst out into a whine of pain. (11) His body shook with a palsy of fright and in shame and rage he felt the scalding cry come from his throat and the scalding tears falling out of his eyes and down his flaming cheeks. . . .

(12) Stephen knelt down quickly pressing his beaten hands to his sides. (13) To think of them beaten and swollen with pain all in a moment made him feel so sorry for them as if they were not his own but someone else's that he felt sorry for. (14) And as he knelt, calming the last sobs in his throat and feeling the burning tingling pain pressed in to his sides, he thought of the hands which he had held out in the air with the palms up and of the firm touch of the prefect of studies when he had steadied the shaking fingers and of the beaten swollen reddened mass of palm and fingers that shook helplessly in the air.*

COMMENT: *Joyce achieves effectiveness in this description through brilliant diction. As a result, he doesn't merely describe: he re-creates the experience. Notice how words like "scalding," "palsy," "trembling," "stinging," "tingling," and "quivering" make the whole painful affair come to life again, first in the mind and memory of the author, and then in the mind of the reader.*

definition, description

Look up the meaning of onomatopoeia. Do you find any examples of this in the passage?

Note the attention to minute detail. The senses are keenly alive: Not only does Stephen suffer; the reader suffers as well.

Do not miss the use of metaphor ("like a leaf in the fire," "the loud crack of a broken stick") and of repetition (a pivotal word like "scalding" appears again and again).

Good prose style has variety in kind and length of sentences. The twelfth sentence has eleven words; the thirteenth, thirty-five; the fourteenth, seventy-three.

III

I define as most seriously overpopulated that nation whose people by virtue of their numbers and activities are most rapidly decreasing the ability of the land to support human life. With our large population, our affluence and our technological monstrosities the United States wins first place by a substantial margin.

Let's compare the US to India, for example. We have 203 million people, whereas she has 540 million on much less land. But look at the impact of people on the land.

The average Indian eats his daily few cups of rice (or perhaps wheat, whose production on American farms contributed to our one percent per year drain in quality of our active farmland), draws his bucket of water from the communal well and sleeps in a mud hut. In his daily rounds to gather cow dung to burn to cook his rice and warm his feet, his footsteps, along with those of millions of his countrymen, help bring about a slow deterioration of the ability of the land to support people. His contribution to the destruction of the land is minimal.

An American, on the other hand, can be expected to destroy a piece of land on which he builds a home, garage and driveway. He will contribute his share to the 142 million tons of smoke and fumes, seven million junked cars, 20 million tons of paper, 48 billion cans, and 26 billion bottles the overburdened environment must absorb each year. To run his air conditioner we will strip-mine a Kentucky hillside, push the dirt and slate down into the stream, and burn coal in a power generator, whose smokestack contributes to a plume of smoke massive enough to cause cloud seeding and premature precipitation from Gulf winds which should be irrigating the wheat farms of Minnesota.

In his lifetime he will personally pollute three million gallons of water, and industry and agriculture will use ten times this much water in his behalf. To provide these needs the US Army Corps of Engineers will build dams and flood farmland. He will also use 21,000 gallons of leaded gasoline containing boron, drink 28,000 pounds of milk and eat 10,000 pounds of meat. The latter is produced and squandered in a life pattern unknown to Asians. A steer on a Western range eats plants containing minerals necessary for plant life. Some of these are incorporated into the body of the steer which is later shipped for slaughter. After being eaten by man these nutrients are flushed down the toilet into the ocean or buried in the cemetery, the surface of which is cluttered with boulders called tombstones and has been removed from productivity. The result is a continual drain on the productivity of range land. Add to this the erosion of overgrazed lands, and the effects of the falling water table as we mine Pleistocene deposits of groundwater to irrigate to produce food for more people, and we can see why our land is dying far more rapidly than did the great civilizations of the Middle East, which experienced the same cycle. The average Indian citizen, whose fecal material goes back to the land, has but a minute fraction of the destructive effect on the land that the affluent American does.*

> COMMENT: *Wayne Davis wishes to define for us the concepts of overpopulation and affluence. For his definition he relies heavily on illustration, comparison and contrast. Keeping in mind that the above paragraphs are only part of an article, do you think that he will be able to defend his thesis that "our affluence rests on a crumbling foundation"? Read the entire article before making a final decision.*

IV

The suburb has long had a powerful hold on the American imagination. In the national mythology it is a place of status and security; it is the persistent dream of a green and pleasant oasis not too far from the office, a plot of ground that offers the calm of the country with all the advantages of the city within easy reach. The dream ranges from the manicured privacy of Long Island's "Gold Coast" to the die-stamped uniformity of California's Daly City, which inspired Malvana Reynolds' derisive song *Little Boxes*. Between those extremes hovers a world of split levels and power mowers, station wagons and shopping centers, kaffeeklatsches and barbecue pits. "Most Americans are not urbanites," observes Sociologist Herbert Gans (*The Levittowners*) of the Harvard-M.I.T. Joint Center for Urban Studies. "The one-family home is something everyone aspires to, and the best place to get it is in the suburbs." **

*Wayne H. Davis, "Overpopulated America," *The New Republic* (January 10, 1970). Reprinted by permission of the author.
** *Time* magazine, March 15, 1971, from "Suburbia: The New American Plurality." Reprinted by permission from *Time*, The Weekly Newsmagazine; Copyright Time, Inc. 1971.

definition, description

COMMENT: *This lead paragraph proceeds mainly by means of*
detail and instances. "[It] is a place" and "it is the persistent
dream" help to reveal the authors' method early in the paragraph.
"Between those extremes" ushers in a brief, selective catalogue of
the diversified items one can find in suburbia. The paragraph ends
with an appropriate, telling quotation by a sociologist.

V

The stage in Shakespeare's time was a naked room with a blanket for
a curtain; but he made it a field for monarchs. That law of unity, which
has its foundations, not in the factitious necessity of custom, but in nature
itself, the unity of feeling, is every where and at all times observed by
Shakespeare in his plays. Read Romeo and Juliet—all is youth and
spring;—youth with its follies, its virtues, its precipitancies;—spring with
its odours, its flowers, and its transiency; it is one and the same feeling
that commences, goes through, and ends the play. The old men, the
Capulets and the Montagues, are not common old men; they have an
eagerness, a heartiness, a vehemence, the effect of spring; with Romeo,
his change of passion, his sudden marriage, and his rash death, are all
the effects of youth;—whilst in Juliet love has all that is tender and melan-
choly in the nightingale, all that is voluptuous in the rose, with whatever
is sweet in the freshness of spring; but it ends with a long deep sigh like
the last breeze of the Italian evening. This unity of feeling and character
pervades every drama of Shakespeare.*

COMMENT: *Coleridge gives a romantic description of Shakespeare's*
stage or, more accurately, drama. One suspects that he is airing
his own ideas of life and characters rather than Shakespeare's.
Nevertheless, it is a grand exercise in lyrical prose. A student who
attempts the same kind of writing must be careful lest he becomes
too lush.

VI

"What is REAL?" asked the Rabbit one day, when they were lying side
by side near the nursery fender, before Nana came to tidy the room. "Does
it mean having things that buzz inside you and a stick-out handle?"

"Real isn't how you are made," said the Skin Horse. "It's a thing that

*S. T. Coleridge, from *Literary Remains*, 1836–39.

happens to you. When a child loves you for a long, long time, not just to play with, but REALLY loves you, then you become Real."

"Does it hurt?" asked the Rabbit.

"Sometimes," said the Skin Horse, for he was always truthful. "When you are Real you don't mind being hurt."

"Does it happen all at once, like being wound up," he asked, "or bit by bit?"

"It doesn't happen all at once," said the Skin Horse. "You become. It takes a long time. That's why it doesn't often happen to people who break easily, or have sharp edges, or who have to be carefully kept. Generally, by the time you are Real, most of your hair has been loved off, and your eyes drop out and you get loose in the joints and very shabby. But these things don't matter at all, because once you are Real you can't be ugly, except to people who don't understand."

. . . The Rabbit sighed. He thought it would be a long time before this magic called Real happened to him. He longed to become Real, to know what it felt like; and yet the idea of growing shabby and losing his eyes and whiskers was rather sad. He wished that he could become it without these uncomfortable things happening to him.*

COMMENT: *Custom tells us that in recording conversation we should indicate each change of speaker with a new paragraph. As far as sense and not merely external form are concerned, however, the preceding lines may be considered as one paragraph only. It moves along by defining; but in so doing it presents sly argumentation and dramatic development.*

VII

Drama, unlike other kinds of literature, is written not primarily to be read by an individual reader but to be presented on a stage by actors for the entertainment of an audience, and hence to attract mass responses. This objective conditions its nature and structure. The major aim of drama, like that of the other arts, is aesthetic in that it attempts to move people emotionally, to arouse their interests, and to satisfy those interests. The interests and the satisfactions may be on a relatively low aesthetic level, and a play may be merely the temporary amusement of an idle hour; or the interests satisfied, and hence the play, may be on a level as high as that attained by any art. On the highest level drama is a primal means of ordering human existence, of interpreting life, and of giving it meaning.

* Margery Williams, from *The Velveteen Rabbit.* Reprinted by permission of Doubleday & Company, Inc.

It is one of the chief instruments through which man has attempted to explore and explain his own nature. Its history from the time of the Greeks to the present is a record of the changing conceptions of human nature. It provides us with no less than a universal picture of the nature of man, individual man and social man, ludicrous man and noble man, good man and evil man. The average individual in a single lifetime, even with the widest possible acquaintance, can come to know intimately relatively few human beings, and directly from this experience it is not possible to understand the vast complexities of human nature and the wide potentials of human conduct. An intimate knowledge of dramatic literature gives an additional dimension of experience in knowing man and his capacities for feeling, thought, and action. Drama is an ideal means to this under-standing, for it has something of the universal appeal that music has: in one or another of its forms, everyone can enjoy and appreciate it. And in performance, drama can be in some degree experienced by even those who do not comprehend its words. To see how drama gives us insight into man and his conduct, it is necessary to examine in some detail the chief aspects of its nature and structure.*

> COMMENT: *Here again we have a paragraph that could be divided into two. Where would you make this division? Why? The paragraph will stand close analysis, for it is carefully organized. Note how smoothly Heffner steps from one idea to another. There are no sudden jars, no bewildering gaps. It is easy to follow his process of thinking as he talks about the objective of drama, about its low, higher and highest levels, about the nature of the related experi-ence. The last sentence anticipates the forthcoming explanation.*

VIII

The Kaibab squirrel is of about the same size as the well-known grey squirrel, or a little longer. Its back is a dark grizzled grey, with a tinge of reddish-brown from rump to shoulders. It has black under parts. Its ears have prominent black tufts; its large, bushy tail . . . is white, with an indistinct greyish stripe running along the centre of its upper side.**

> COMMENT: *A real challenge for the student is to describe in keen, specific detail any animal he has met in the woods, at a zoo, any-where. What is his color, weight, body characteristics? Or for that matter, he should try to describe in minute detail any tree that he sees on campus. It is not as easy as it may seem at first.*

* Hubert Heffner, from *The Nature of Drama.* Reprinted by permission of Houghton Mifflin Co.
** James Fisher, Noel Simon, Jack Vincent, et al., *Wildlife in Danger.* Reprinted by permission of Viking Press.

THE PARAGRAPH OF ILLUSTRATION
AND EXAMPLE

Introduction

A thin line separates definition from illustration, as the paragraphs in the preceding section and in this section clearly reveal. But there is some difference nonetheless. To define, as we have seen, means to set limits to; to illustrate means to make clear, or to provide with pictures and designs. Often, illustration throws light upon what has already been defined or discussed in general terms. For instance, a paragraph about the selfishness of a medieval king could be illustrated by a descriptive cartoon depicting him eating a nineteen-pound turkey while two hundred starving children grovel at his feet.

The paragraph of illustration and example trains the writer to be concrete and specific—and nothing is more important than that. Let us say you are asked to describe Sean O'Brien. You could answer that he is mean, contemptible, and inconsiderate. But you would be much more effective if you illustrated his qualities. Catalogue his routine on a typical day: Sean leaves home at 8:30 in the morning, after beating his wife and refusing to buy bread for his seven children. As he turns the corner, a blind, eighty-year-old woman asks him to help her across the street. Sean ignores her. At that moment, a cat crosses in front of him. Sean kicks it. He then hails a taxi. "Step on it, driver," he yells, as he enters the cab. "Why don't you watch where you're going?" he shouts a moment later as the driver narrowly misses another car. When he enters his office, his secretary hands him a special delivery from his mother. She is alone in Outer Mongolia, homeless, penniless, hopelessly maimed. Would he please send a few of his million dollars to help her. Sean files the letter, only half-read, in the waste basket. But why continue? By this time even the least astute can surmise that Sean is indeed mean and contemptible. Description, yes; illustration, certainly.

The paragraph of example follows the same line of development. It substantiates a statement by providing a typical and representative instance. The paragraph may begin like this: "I know that Louise is not completely honest. Last year, for example, she cheated on her income tax. The year before that she robbed the First National Bank." For instance, *Time* magazine may talk about "middle Americans" by telling us of their attitude toward campus dissent, their flags of assertive patriotism, their decals and ideological totems, their political inclinations and religious tendencies, their attitude toward art and art forms. At the end of *Time's* description and illustration we have a definite idea of what the term "middle Americans" means.

I

KNOWLEDGE is increasing so fast, a recent ad said, that the problem of education is to find better ways "to pack it into young heads." This popular belief is wrong, and causes much of what is so wrong with our schools. For years, it is true, learned men used their brains to store and retrieve information. Today, the child who has been taught in school to stuff his head with facts, recipes, this-is-how-you-do-it, is obsolete even before he leaves the building. Anything he can do, or be taught to do, a machine can do, and soon will do, better and cheaper.

    note that nature of idea calls for explanation

    history

    items of illustration

What children need, even just to make a living, are qualities that can never be trained into a machine-inventiveness, flexibility, resourcefulness, curiosity and, above all, judgment.

    qualities are itemized

The chief products of schooling these days are not these qualities, not even the knowledge and skills they try to produce, but stupidity, ignorance, incompetence, self-contempt, alienation, apathy, powerlessness, resentment and rage. We can't afford such products any longer. The purpose of education can no longer be to turn out people who know a few facts, a few skills and who will always believe and do what they are told. We need big changes, and in a hurry. . . .*

    more illustration

    next two sentences are transitional

* John Holt, "Why We Need New Schooling." Copyright 1970 by *Look*. Reprinted by permission of the author.

II

Pathetic fallacy was a phrase invented by John Ruskin in 1856 to designate the description of an inanimate object as though it had human capacities and feelings (*Modern Painters,* Vol. III, Part iv). As used by Ruskin the term was derogatory, since it applied, he said, not to the "true appearances of things to us," but to "the extraordinary, or false appearances, when we are under the influence of emotion, or contemplative fancy." Two of his examples are

> The spendthrift crocus, bursting through the mould
> Naked and shivering, with his cup of gold,

and Coleridge's

> The one red leaf, the last of its clan,
> That dances as often as dance it can.

These passages, Ruskin says, however beautiful, are untrue and "morbid"; in the greatest poets, the pathetic fallacy occurs rarely, and only at a point beyond which it would be inhuman to resist the pressure of the feelings to humanize the facts of perception.

Ruskin's criterion, however, would make the greatest poets, including Shakespeare, "morbid." His term is now used, for the most part, as a neutral way to define a very common poetic phenomenon. "The pathetic fallacy" is applied especially to passages in which the attribution of human traits to natural objects is more unobtrusive and less formal than in the figure known as *personification.**

COMMENT: Note that the paragraph begins with a definition of pathetic fallacy. This obviously is not enough. The author, therefore, quickly gives a few examples. The word however *in the last paragraph is important, for it indicates that now neither Ruskin's definition nor his examples will serve.*

III

To the casual eye, she must have seemed a foolish, if not a downright ridiculous woman. She was full of airs and graces that were faintly grotesque considering the lowly orbit in which she moved; but apart from her obsession, which was pathological and worsened with the years, she was extremely intelligent. It is both sad and strange that this often silly woman, dressed usually in a most idiotic attire, was in fact an immensely shrewd and sensitive human being. The two are not mutually exclusive. I sat in a theatre a few years ago at the out-of-town opening of a now famous play and watched, fascinated and puzzled, as the actress on the stage played out the tragic destiny of the playwright's imagining. There was something about the character of this woman on the stage that tolled the bell of remembrance within me. It was almost as though I had known this woman myself—echo after echo reminded me of someone I had known in my own life—and suddenly I knew who it was I was remembering. Aunt Kate. The play that brought her back to me so sharply was *A Streetcar Named Desire* and the character was the unforgettable Blanche Du Bois. I do not mean to suggest that the story of Blanche was my aunt's story or that she was anything like the twisted and tormented Blanche; but there was enough of Blanche in my Aunt Kate—a touching combination of the sane and the ludicrous along with some secret splendor within herself—that re-awakened long-forgotten memories. I think Tennessee Williams would have understood my Aunt Kate at once—perhaps far better than I did, for in those early years I confess I was a little ashamed of her. She was too strange a figure for the conforming little beasts that children usually are for me to have been completely comfortable about her. I always looked straight ahead when we passed other children that I knew in the street and swallowed my discomfort as best I could.*

> COMMENT: *This is a fine example of how thin the line between description and illustration can become. Moss Hart sets off to illustrate the "foolishness" and "ridiculousness" of his aunt. He continues by telling what she did and how she looked. The allusion to Blanche Du Bois, especially for those acquainted with the play, is particularly illuminating. There are few transitional phrases or words in the sentence, yet the paragraph has an admirable coherence. How does the author achieve this?*

IV

At least since the days [of] Voltaire and the Encyclopedistes we have all been conditioned to suppose that the French, as people and as writers, are preeminently limpid thinkers. This is assumed almost as carelessly as the idea that the Germans are profusely unintelligible, the Swiss hygienically boring, the Americans excessively interested in status-seeking and the Swedes addicted to suicide. The essentially clear-minded, sparkling

---

*Moss Hart, from *Act I,* copyright 1959 by Random House, Inc. By permission of the publisher and Martin Secker & Warburg Ltd.

Frenchman is a popular and a sophisticated cliché. Although it is more subtle and more justifiable historically, it corresponds to the vulgar French version of the Englishman as a Colonel Bramble or a Major Thompson. A School-master ploughing through Racine with his pupils or a lecturer describing the intricacies of the Common Market to a group of Rotarians will refer to French clearness with equal enthusiasm.

Innumerable Frenchmen, especially intellectuals or those who think of themselves as such, are still convinced that they have a superior position in the world as regards the manipulation of ideas. In *The Ideal Reader* (recently published in England) one finds Jacques Riviere asserting that

> French intelligence has no equal; no other is more powerful, more keen, more profound. . . . It is the only intelligence that still exists in the world of today.

In 1962 nobody in Paris would dare to write this kind of thing straightforwardly. Yet many French writers would feel that it is basically true and that this monopoly of intelligence has been a rightful privilege since Cartesianism. This reputation is cherished as much as that attached to French cuisine and wines. Any attempt to question it is dismissed with the supposedly damning and ultimate rebukes: "scientiste," "positiviste," "empiriciste"!*

COMMENT: Do not miss the transitional pattern in these two paragraphs. Beginning with sentence two, the author spells off a list of clichés. The last two sentences in the first paragraph give contrasting examples of clichés among the British and French. The quotation from The Ideal Reader *gives an added strength to what is being stated as a fact. Even though the author by the end of these two paragraphs has not begun to explode the myth of French clarity, we can anticipate that he will do so.*

V

If we look more closely at the fiction produced by southern writers, we shall find a cause for much of the similarity so basic as to be self-evident, but often overlooked for the simple reason that many readers and critics of southern fiction have never lived in the South. The materials of this body of fiction are regional, and they are based on what sociologists, for example Howard Odum in *An American Epoch*, have called a powerful folk society and culture in a period of transition. The physical and cultural

* The Times Literary Supplement: from "The Myth of Clarity." Reprinted from The Times Literary Supplement, London, by permission.

environment are similar: from the work of many authors we become familiar with the red clay farms, the cotton fields, the hills and forests, the primitive farm houses, the small hamlets with their post offices, general stores, courthouses, banks, churches, all of which serve as communal gathering spots. We become familiar with the porches where small groups collect on summer afternoons and evenings to tell and retell legends out of the local past, events out of the present. And we know the sound of their voices speaking.

Furthermore, these southern communities consist of a wide variety of classes and types of people who are both plainly and subtly stratified within and among their larger or smaller groupings—white and Negroes, farmers and townsfolk, professional and business people, "cultured" and "common," landowners and sharecroppers, Methodists and Baptists. Yet all live in the greatest intimacy, with much factual and intuitive knowledge about each other, with a widely shared core of attitudes and beliefs. The southern writer is party to all this, mixing and sharing in the life of the southern community, which is not particularly conscious of or impressed by his being a writer. In a sense the southern writer of fiction has only to see and record, to listen and write "by ear."*

> COMMENT: The first paragraph makes explicit reference to one example taken from Howard Odum; however, the whole paragraph as well as the next can be taken as a good specimen of development by illustration and example. The cataloging technique (farms, post offices, stores, churches, etc.) is especially characteristic of this kind of development. The final result is a picture that accounts for much of the similarity of materials among southern writers.

VI

The true nature of tradition—as a growing, organic phenomenon—is often ignored by some teachers. As a consequence, much to their own unwitting darkness, they condemn as non-traditional works that are in an intrinsic sense most traditional. Let us look at a few examples of this mistake. T. S. Eliot, for instance, is still condemned by some as a new poet who is much too radical and obscure. (By this time, of course, Eliot is as old to students of the 70's as Browning and Hardy were to undergraduates of the 20's and 30's.) Only in a senseless view was Eliot new even in the 20's. He built on tradition, ancient forms, cultures, literatures, myths. It is ironic to note that what is passé for undergraduates today

* Ruth M. Vande Kieft, from *Eudora Welty*. Reprinted by permission of Ruth M. Vande Kieft and Twayne Publishing Co., Inc.

may have been "passed-over" by their teachers. So also many narrow-bond traditionalists have nothing but sweeping condemnation for impressionistic art; yet artists who should know tell us that impressionism is in a way a return to Renaissance representationalism. It may have a different approach, they explain, but is has the same objective and ideal. Brubeck is a jazz artist, and jazz is new (at least to our friend, the traditionalist). Therefore, off with Brubeck's head. But what are the facts? Brubeck is a gifted musician using devices and techniques borrowed from Bach. So also, the early Stan Kenton leaned heavily on the same eighteenth-century composer. Instances in music, architecture, literature, painting could be multiplied, showing that what is condemned simply because it is new is not new at all. Let us glance at one final instance that, we hope, is not typical but does illustrate how ludicrous the traditionalistic attitude can become. Recently at a nearby college a teacher was confronted by an apoplectic confrere: "What about this e.e. cummings? He doesn't use capitals. This undermines everything we should be teaching in school. How can we expect our children to punctuate when our poets don't?" The teacher was tempted to explain that Old Testament Hebrew not only ignored the distinction between capital and small letters, but also violated proper direction by writing backward instead of forward. As a gentleman, however, he resisted the temptation and left his confrere ignorant but secure in his critical limbo.

COMMENT: There is an old dictum that tells us never to argue about facts; all we have to do is to make certain that they are correct. Thus, if we are to puncture the balloon of narrow traditionalism, we must look to the facts about modern creativity. In this paragraph, the most deflating fact is saved for the end.

THE PARAGRAPH OF COMPARISON, CONTRAST, ANALOGY

Introduction

Let us suppose you are asked to write three expository paragraphs on Mary Fachette. After you are finished, your classmate should be able to identify Miss Fachette even though he has never met her; he should have conclusive evidence of her outstanding virtue; finally, he should be able to judge whether she's attractive or unattractive. Your first paragraph could be developed by description: by detailing her facial features, her size, the color of her hair, her complexion, and so forth. Your second paragraph could be developed by illustration: noting that she donated one hundred dollars to the Red Cross last month, nursed her invalid mother, sympathetically listened to her neighbor's woes. Your third and last paragraph might be one of comparison and contrast: comparing her hair with Raquel Welch's, her eyes with Venessa Redgrave's, her nose with Barbra Streisand's. In effect, you help the reader to visualize the unknown Mary Fachette by placing her beside certain women who are known.

The paragraph of comparison, contrast, and analogy uses an old but simple pedagogical device: revelation of the unknown through the known. If someone has never seen an elephant, we can enlighten him by comparing or contrasting its hide with that of the rhinoceros, its size with that of a horse, and continuing with what it is like and unlike until he has acquired a fairly accurate notion of the animal.

While comparison shows similarities between two objects or actions, analogy shows their resemblance in so far as attributes, effects or conditions are concerned. Thus, Christ makes an analogy between himself and a man who goes out to sow seed, not because the farmer looks or speaks like Christ (although he may), but because the seed that the farmer sows falls upon different kinds of ground and does or does not bear fruit even as the word of God that Christ distributes falls on various kinds of men and does or does not bear fruit. Kierkegaard, in the example given below, gives us a comparison between the prophet Nathan and King David. The prophet's words that follow contain one of the most telling analogies in the Bible. Finally, we must remember that all analogies have limitations. Thus, Mortimer Adler's analogy of baseball and reading sheds a great deal of light on one occupation by revealing its resemblance to the other. But Adler goes on to point out that, while baseball and reading may be alike in some respects, in most respects they are utterly different.

I

Then one day there came a prophet to King David. Let us make the situation vivid to us and modernize it a little. The one is the king, the man who has the highest rank in the nation; the other a prophet, a man much esteemed in the nation—both of them of course men of culture, and one may be sure that their intercourse with one another, their conversation, will bear unmistakably the marks of culture. *Besides,* they were both, and one of them more especially, celebrated authors. King David was the renowned poet, and, as a natural consequence of this, a connoisseur, and elegant arbiter of good taste, who knew how to appreciate the form of presentation, the choice of expressions, and the construction of a poem, the linguistic form and the cadence, and whether it was favorable or prejudicial to morals.

And it is a lucky meeting, just the right man to come to; for the prophet had composed a "novella," a story which he would fain have the honor of reciting before his Majesty, the crowned poet and connoisseur of poetry.

"There dwelt two men in one city, the one rich, and the other poor. The rich man had flocks and herds in great abundance; but the poor man had nothing except one little ewe lamb, which he had bought and raised; and it grew up together with him and his children; it ate of his own meat and drank of his own cup, and lay in his bosom and was like a daughter to him. *And* there came a traveller unto the rich man; and, in order to make a feast for his guest, he was unwilling to take from his own herd. *Instead,* he robbed the poor man of his lamb and dressed for the feast."

transitional—note narrative form

differences and likenesses begin

**transitional
setting stage for story**

transitional—whole paragraph serves as transition to the story

analogy begins

poor man and rich man will not be identified until the end

transitional

transitional

David, burning with indignation at the wrong, said to Nathan, "As the Lord is a living God, death is the penalty for such a man as this; for this cruel deed he shall make recompense fourfold." And Nathan said to David, "*Thou art the man.*"*

David takes the bait

Note dramatic and climactic finish

COMMENT: *Even if you did not know beforehand the story of David and Bathsheba, would you be able to infer what had happened from Nathan's analogy? In what way is the analogy effective? Does the resemblance between David and the rich man break down at any place? Why didn't Nathan tell David directly that God was displeased with him? Kierkegaard notes that both David and Nathan were literary men. Does Nathan tell a story merely because he knows David will be entranced by its literary merit?*

II

Let me use the example of baseball. Catching the ball is just as much an activity as pitching or hitting it. The pitcher or batter is the giver here in the sense that his activity initiates the motion of the ball. The catcher or fielder is the receiver in the sense that his activity terminates it. Both are equally active, though the activities are distinctly different. If anything is passive here, it is the ball: it is pitched and caught. It is the inert thing which is put in motion or stopped, whereas the living men are active, moving to pitch, hit, or catch. The analogy with writing and reading is almost perfect. The thing which is written and read, like the ball, is the passive object in some way common to the two activities which begin and terminate the process.

We can go a step farther with this analogy. A good catcher is one who stops the ball which has been hit or pitched. The art of catching is the skill of knowing how to do this as well as possible in every situation. So the art of reading is the skill of catching every sort of communication as well as possible. But the reader as "catcher" is more like the fielder than the man behind the plate. The catcher signals for a particular pitch. He knows what to expect before the ball is thrown. Not so, however, in the case of the batter and fielder. Fielders may wish that batters would obey signals from them, but that isn't the way the game is played. So readers

---

*Soren Kierkegaard, from *Self-Examination* (1851), translated by Walter Lowrie. Reprinted by permission of Princeton University Press.

may sometimes wish that writers would submit completely to their desires for reading matter, but the facts are usually otherwise. The reader has to go after what comes out into the field.

The analogy breaks down at two points, both of which are instructive. In the first place, the batter and the fielder being on opposite sides, do not have the same end in view. Each thinks of himself as successful only if he frustrates the other. In contrast, pitcher and catcher are successful only to the extent that they co-operate. Here the relation of writer and reader is more like that between the men on the battery. The writer certainly isn't trying not to be caught, although the reader may often think so. Successful communication occurs in any case where what the writer wanted to have received finds its way into the reader's possession. The writer's and the reader's skill converge upon a common end.

In the second place, the ball is a simple unit. It is either completely caught or not. A piece of writing, however, is a complex object. It can be received more or less completely, all the way from very little of what the writer intended to the whole thing. The amount the reader gets will usually depend on the amount of activity he puts into the process, as well as upon the skill with which he executes the different mental acts that are involved.

Now we can define the second criterion for judging reading ability. Given the same thing to read, one man reads it better than another, first, by reading it more actively, and second, by performing each of the acts involved more successfully. These two things are related. Reading is a complex activity, just as writing is. It consists of a large number of separate acts, all of which must be performed in a good reading. Hence, the man who can perform more of these various acts is better able to read.*

COMMENT: *This passage will reward careful study. In the first paragraph, Adler stresses the resemblances between baseball and writing, concluding that the analogy is almost perfect. The second paragraph continues with resemblances but notes something that is different. What sentence indicates this turning point? Could the third and fourth paragraphs be combined into one? Why? Note the first sentence of each paragraph, and especially of the last three. How do they contribute to the organization of what Adler wishes to say? Transitional words and phrases (but, however, in the first place, in contrast, in the second place, now) abound throughout the passage. Underline as many as you can find. Read the passage omitting these transitional elements. In what way is it now changed?*

* Mortimer J. Adler, from *How to Read a Book.* Copyright 1940 by Mortimer J. Adler. Reprinted by permission of Simon and Shuster, Inc.

III

While no actor can be a star, it should be admitted that a few stars did get a chance to prove they could act. Though only perfecting her stardom in *Jezebel*, when Miss Davis played the naive girl in *The Petrified Forest* she showed that she had range as an actress. Humphrey Bogart did the same thing in *The Treasure of the Sierra Madre* and *The African Queen*. But for many stars—John Wayne is a prime example—the most daring departure from the routine of stardom has been a few late films that are parodies of their own early work. Dustin Hoffman knows he's only an actor. He even flaunts this self-awareness by admiring the fact that the lead is no longer so important to the public as a film's director or script content. An acid test for identifying a star, as opposed to a mere actor, is that any stand-up comic who's not tone deaf can do imitations of stars. Try doing an imitation of Dustin Hoffman.*

> COMMENT: *The author presumes an elementary knowledge of "stars" and "actors" current and within history. He makes a subtle, but telling distinction between the two. Even without knowing the complete article, and perhaps without knowing all the names mentioned, do you agree with his contrast? From your knowledge of movies, can you make your own contrast?*

IV

One [variant] is the late capitalist, and hence late, late Calvinist, economic development known as planned obsolescence. There are two basic interpretations of planned obsolescence, one optimistic and generally put out by the people who practice it, the other pessimistic and adhered to by the people who suffer from that theory of production. The optimistic view is that every day in every way our industrial production gets better and better and therefore the consumer who purchased, say, a super-eight dodecahedron special last year will naturally want to trade it in for a superduper model this year. The process releases last year's model back to the market, making work for used-car salesmen and allowing citizens a rung or two down the ladder to taste of last year's luxe. The pessimistic version, on the other hand, has it that American industry is run by a bunch of planning obsoleters whose job it is to design things so that they will fall apart the day after the warranty expires and thus maintain a lively demand for replacements.**

---

* Colin L. Westerbeck, "The Importance of Being Oscar." Copyright 1971 by *Commonweal*. Reprinted by permission of the publisher.
** Frank Getlein, "Mad Dogs and Who Go Out in the Mid-day Sun?" Copyright 1971 by *Commonweal*. Reprinted by permission of the publisher.

COMMENT: This paragraph is a carefully structured analysis of two divergent views of planned obsolescence, a highly debatable subject. Two sides of one topic can often be presented in such a manner that each will illuminate the other.

V

Still, they pursue this aim by very different courses. The uppermost idea with *Hellenism* is to see things as they really are; the uppermost idea with *Hebraism* is conduct and obedience. Nothing can do away with this ineffaceable difference. The Greek quarrel with the body and its desires is, that they hinder right thinking; the Hebrew quarrel with them is, that they hinder right acting. "He that keepeth the law, happy is he"; "Blessed is the man that feareth the Eternal, that delighteth greatly in his commandments;"—that is the Hebrew notion of felicity; and, pursued with passion and tenacity, this notion would not let the Hebrew rest till, as is well known, he had at last got out of the law a network of prescriptions to enwrap his whole life, to govern every movement of it, every impulse, every action. The Greek notion of felicity, *on the other hand,* is perfectly conveyed in these words of a great French moralist: "C'est le bonheur des hommes," *— when? when they abhor that which is evil?—no; when they exercise themselves in the law of the Lord day and night?—no; when they die daily?—no; when they walk about the New Jerusalem with palms in their hands?—; but when they think aright, when their thought hits: "*Quand ils pensent juste.*"** *At the bottom of both* the Greek and the Hebrew notion is the desire, native in man, for reason and the will of God, the feeling after the universal order,—in a word, the love of God. But while Hebraism seizes upon certain plain, capital intimations of the universal order, and rivets itself, one may say, with unequalled grandeur of earnestness and intensity on the study and observance of them, the bent of Hellenism is to follow, with flexible activity, the whole play of the universal order, to be apprehensive of missing any part of it, of sacrificing one part to another, to slip away from resting in this or that intimation of it, however capital. An unclouded clearness of mind, an unimpeded play of thought, is what this bent drives at. The governing idea of Hellenism is *spontaneity of consciousness;* that of Hebraism, *strickness of conscience.*†

COMMENT: This paragraph is a combination of two kinds of development: definition and contrast. If we were to punctuate this today,

---

* "This is happiness among men."
** "When they think correctly."
† Matthew Arnold, "Hebraism and Hellenism," from *Culture and Anarchy* (1868).

*would there by any changes? Are the longer sentences hard to fol-
low? Could you rewrite them making them clearer but without losing any part of Arnold's ideas?*

VI

Now, it is clear that the decline of a language must ultimately have
political and economic causes: it is not due simply to the bad influence
of this or that individual writer. But an effect can become a cause, rein-
forcing the original cause and producing the same effect in an intensified
form, and so on indefinitely. A man may take to drink because he feels
himself to be a failure, and then fail all the more completely because he
drinks. It is rather the same thing that is happening to the English language. It becomes ugly and inaccurate because our thoughts are foolish,
but the slovenliness of our language makes it easier for us to have foolish
thoughts. The point is that the process is reversible. Modern English,
especially written English, is full of bad habits which spread by imitation
and which can be avoided if one is willing to take the necessary trouble.
If one gets rid of these habits one can think more clearly, and to think
clearly is a necessary first step towards political regeneration: so that the
fight against bad English is not frivolous and is not the exclusive concern
of professional writers . . .*

*COMMENT: The cause–effect–cause relationship of the decline
of a language is forcefully brought out by analogy of the cause-
effect–cause pattern of a drinker. Orwell presumes that his readers
can elaborate on an analogy that is simply mentioned.*

VII

Once there was a lady who was completely surrounded by her enemies,
her land all laid waste, and she herself destitute in an earthly castle. But
a king of great power loved her so much that he sent messengers to her
one after another, and many times several at once, with many fair jewels,
and with food to sustain her. He also sent an army to help her hold the
castle. She accepted it all in a thoughtless way, and was so hard hearted
that he could never come nearer to her love. What more could he do? At
last he went himself. He showed her the beauty of his face, the face of

---

*George Orwell, *Shooting an Elephant and Other Essays.* Reprinted by permission of Harcourt
Brace Jovanovich, Inc. and A. M. Heath & Company Ltd.

one who was of all men fairest to behold. He spoke words to her with such tenderness and such delight that they could have raised the dead to life. He worked many wonders and great miracles before her; he revealed to her the power he had and told her of his kingdom. Finally, he offered to make her queen of all he possessed. But to no avail. Was not all this disdain strange? For she was not worthy to be his servant. But love had so overwhelmed his heart that he said, "Lady, you are being attacked, your enemies are so strong that you cannot hope to escape from them without my help, which can prevent their putting you to a disgraceful death after your suffering. For love of you I shall take this fight upon myself and deliver you from those who would kill you. I know without any doubt that I will receive a mortal wound from them, but I shall meet it gladly if only to win your heart. Now I beg you, for the love I show you, that you love me in return, at least after my death since you do not love me while I live." The king carried all of this out, rescued her from her enemies, and was himself outrageously tortured and finally slain. But by a miracle he rose from death to life. Would not this lady be of an evil nature if she did not love him thereafter above everything else?*

COMMENT: *The author of this famous guide for anchoresses is making an analogy between a fairy tale and the story of Christian redemption. He goes on to interpret the analogy; but, even though you may not have read his explication, you should be able to understand the analogy and apply it to the history of mankind.*

VIII

In consequence of hearing so much about an Omniscient God, a being of supernatural wisdom and penetration who was always with us, who made, in fact, a fourth in our company, I had come to think of Him, not without awe, but with absolute confidence. My Father and Mother, in their serene discipline of me, never argued with one another, never even differed; their wills seemed absolutely one. My mother always deferred to my Father and in his absence spoke of him to me, as if he were all-wise. I confused him in some sense with God; at all events I believed that my Father knew everything and saw everything. One morning in my sixth year, my Mother and I were alone in the morning-room, when my Father came in and announced some fact to us. I was standing on the rug, gazing at him, and when he made this statement, I remember turning quickly, in embarrassment, and looking into the fire. The shock to me was as that of a

*Anonymous, The Ancrene Riwle (c. 1225).

thunderbolt, for what my Father had said "was not true." My Mother and I, who had been present at the trifling incident, were aware that it had not happened exactly as it had been reported to him. My Mother gently told him so, and he accepted the correction. Nothing could possibly have been more trifling to my parents, but to me it meant an epoch. Here was the appalling discovery, never suspected before, that my Father was not as God, and did not know everything. The shock was not caused by any suspicion that he was not telling the truth, as it appeared to him, but by the awful proof that he was not, as I had supposed, omniscient.*

COMMENT: *Mr. Gosse dramatizes a young boy's moment of discovery. A situation, initiated as a foregone conclusion, an accepted and dogmatic fact, becomes a revelation through an episode. Implicit in the paragraph is the contrast between father and Father.*

* Edmund Gosse, *Father and Son.* Copyright 1907 by Charles Scribner's Sons. Reprinted by permission of the publisher.

THE PARAGRAPH OF REASONING

Introduction

To write a paragraph of reasoning with competence and facility is no easy matter: one needs a knowledge of logic, and acquaintance with philosophy, a set of ideals and principles, a familiarity with history, truth, and facts. All we can do here is to suggest the way in which this paragraph is developed. Its mastery will have to come with education, maturity, and experience.

The paragraph of reasoning does not ignore emotion—in fact, for persuasive writing emotional appeal is indispensable. But it relies mostly on the thinking process of human beings. It approaches an idea from a rational viewpoint. It proposes, analyzes, attempts to prove on an intelligent level.

The writer relies especially upon two methods of reasoning: induction and deduction. Induction inspects details and phenomena in order to arrive at a general conclusion: Most of the time, the topic sentence or the generalization will come at the end. Deduction goes in the opposite direction by starting with a generalization or a truth that most people will accept and then illustrating how this is true of a specific point. The topic sentence will ordinarily come at the beginning. Actually, induction and deduction are two different sides of the same coin. Let us illustrate.

You know Raymond Sitwell very well; you know him to be especially considerate and generous. However, you have never approached Ray at four o'clock in the afternoon immediately after he finishes his work for the day. One day you do meet him at this time and for the first time at this time ask him for a loan of five dollars. Ray refuses in no uncertain language. This is unlike Ray, who has never refused you before. The next day you meet him at the same time, make the same request, and get the same reaction. After a while the pattern is established: you can depend on the generosity of Ray in the morning or evening but not in the late afternoon. By the process of induction, you have now arrived at a general conclusion: Raymond Sitwell is not in an indulgent mood at four o'clock. At this point, the process of reasoning is reversed. You now know a general truth about Ray. If in the future you are tempted to ask five dollars of Ray, you will think in this fashion which we call a syllogism: Ray is not generous at four o'clock; it is now four o'clock; therefore, this is not a good time to ask him for money. What we do, in fine, is use the experimental

reasoning

or scientific method of inspecting certain things until we have arrived at a generalization. We then use this generalization to come to a conclusion in a particular case.

For the illustration below, A, B, C, D, E, F, and G represent rubber balls that you have tested in a laboratory. You have discovered that all of these and any others like them bounce. Your generalization is that *all* balls made of rubber bounce. You now look at items 1, 2, 3, 4, 5, 6, and 7. You discover that they are rubber balls. Thus, you conclude, all these items will bounce.

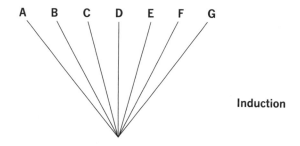

Induction

Generalization: All rubber balls bounce.

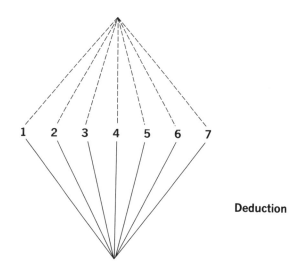

Deduction

Conclusion: Each of these items will bounce.

I

We hold these truths to be self-evident, (1) *that* all men are created equal, (2) *that* they are endowed by their Creator with certain unalienable rights, (3) *that* among these are Life, Liberty, and the pursuit of Happiness. (4) *That* to *secure* these rights, Governments are instituted among Men, deriving their just powers from the consent of the governed. (5) *That whenever* any Form of Government becomes destructive of these ends, *it is the Right of the People to alter it* or to abolish it, and to institute a new Government, laying its foundation on such principles and organizing its powers on such form, as to them shall seem most likely to effect their Safety and Happiness. *Prudence, indeed,* will dictate that Governments long established should not be changed for light and transient causes; and accordingly all experience hath shown, that mankind are more disposed to suffer, while evils are sufferable, than to right themselves by abolishing the forms to which they are accustomed. *But* when a long train of abuses and usurpations, pursuing invariably the same Object evinces a design to reduce them under absolute Despotism, it is their *right,* it is their *duty,* to throw off such Government, and to provide new Guards for their future security.

Such has been the patient sufferance of these Colonies; and such is now the necessity which constrains them to alter their former Systems of Government. The history of the present King of Great Britain is a history of repeated injuries and usurpations, all having in direct object the establishment of an absolute Tyranny over these States. To prove this, let *Facts* be submitted to a candid world.

note tone—determined to convince, to be logical

and sensible

note the five parallel "thats" second part of syllogism is introduced

logical conclusion is reached

anticipates charge of hastiness or imprudence

history of mankind is on side of colonists

notice effective pattern of argument—"but" introduces the factual case

two words provide climax to argument

leading up to illustration of facts—these facts violate the colonists' "unalienable rights" mentioned in first sentence.

He has refused his Assent to Laws, the most wholesome and necessary for the public good.

specific facts strengthen the general statement made at end of first paragraph

He has forbidden his Governors to pass Laws of immediate and pressing importance, unless suspended in their operation till his assent should be obtained; and when so suspended, he has utterly neglected to attend to them.

Jefferson began with deduction—note that here he has changed to induction

He has refused to pass other Laws for the accommodation of large districts of people, unless those people would relinquish the right of Representation in the Legislature, a right inestimable to them and formidable to tyrants only.*

repetition of "he has" makes argument positive and emphatic

II

The American university is in an exceedingly precarious position. The luster of even the most historic and distinguished of universities is fading rapidly. For the first time in the history of this country there is valid reason for wondering whether the university will survive. Alarmism may be the refuge of the timid, but any optimism at this time would be little more than euphoria. The university in America is in the most critical condition of its history.

There are many reasons for this. Most of them arise directly from the university itself, especially from the profoundly dislocative changes during the past quarter century that have led to fragmentation of its authority in society and to near-dissolution of its internal dogma and community. No genuinely intellectual community can possibly exist save in terms of an aristocracy that consists of respect for the best ideas, scholars and teachers, and the proper ranking of these in relation to ideas, teachers and scholars of lesser worth. Nor can any genuinely intellectual community survive without a system of authority, a system made legitimate by its clearly perceived relation to the function or purpose around which community and aristocracy alike are built.**

COMMENT: *There are many and diverse explanations of the "precarious position" of American colleges and universities. Mr. Nisbet*

*Thomas Jefferson, *The Declaration of Independence.*
**Robert A. Nisbet, from *The Degradation of the Academic Dogma,* Basic Books, Inc., Publishers, New York. 1971.

offers one explanation; one that may seem, at first glance, to be conservative. Taking into account that you do not know his full argument from the two paragraphs produced above, can you follow his reasoning? Can you, from this point, propose a different argument, or add to the argument already initiated?

III

Granted that work (and especially paperwork) is thus elastic in its demands on time, it is manifest that there need be little or no relationship between the work to be done and the size of the staff to which it may be assigned. A lack of real activity does not, of necessity, result in leisure. A lack of occupation is not necessarily revealed by a manifest idleness. The thing to be done swells in importance and complexity in a direct ratio with the time to be spent. This fact is widely recognized, but less attention has been paid to its wider implications, more especially in the field of public administration. Politicians and taxpayers have assumed (with occasional phases of doubt) that a rising total in the number of civil servants must reflect a growing volume of work to be done. Cynics, in questioning this belief, have imagined that the multiplication of officials must have left some of them idle or all of them able to work for shorter hours. But this is a matter in which faith and doubt seem equally misplaced. The fact is that the number of the officials and the quantity of the work are not related to each other at all. The rise in the total of those employed is governed by Parkinson's Law and would be much the same whether the volume of the work were to increase, diminish, or even disappear. The importance of Parkinson's Law lies in the fact that it is a law of growth based upon an analysis of the factors by which that growth is controlled.*

COMMENT: In this well known paragraph—famous and notorious—we have the explicit proposal of Parkinson's Law. It is a bold law (theory), buttressed by sharp reasoning. Are you prepared to accept this law? To accept his logic? Could you argue against the law?

IV

This American government,—what is it but a tradition, though a recent one, endeavoring to transmit itself unimpaired to posterity, but each instant losing some of its integrity? It has not the vitality and force of a single

---

*C. Northcote Parkinson, *Parkinson's Law.* Copyright 1957 by Houghton Mifflin Co. Reprinted by permission of the publisher.

living man; for a single man can bend it to his will. It is a sort of wooden gun to the people themselves; and, if ever they should use it in earnest as a real one against each other, it will surely split. But it is not the less necessary for this; for the people must have some complicated machinery or other, and hear its din, to satisfy that idea of government which they have. Governments show thus how successfully men can be imposed on, even impose on themselves, for their own advantage. It is excellent, we must all allow: yet this government never of itself furthered any enterprise, but by the alacrity with which it got out of its way. It does not keep the country free. It does not settle the West. It does not educate. The character inherent in the American people has done all that has been accomplished; and it would have done somewhat more, if the government had not sometimes got in its way. For government is an expedient by which men would fain succeed in letting one another alone; and, as has been said, when it is most expedient, the governed are most let alone by it. Trade and commerce, if they were not made of India rubber, would never manage to bounce over the obstacles which legislators are continually putting in their way; and, if one were to judge these men wholly by the effects of their actions, and not partly by their intentions, they would deserve to be classed and punished with those mischievous persons who put obstructions on the railroads.*

> COMMENT: Thoreau's argument is based on the motto: "That government is best which governs least." He throws down a challenge for the "establishment," "the conservatives," "the liberals," in fact, for everyone. Perhaps, the earnestness and vehemence of his style affects us immediately and deeply. He has an argument to propose and he does so eloquently. We should follow both manner and matter closely.

V

It is not sufficiently realized that the kind of military intervention we have witnessed in the past quarter century is, if not wholly unprecedented, clearly a departure from a long and deeply rooted tradition. Since the Neutrality Proclamation of 1793 that tradition has been one of nonintervention. Washington, and his cabinet, refused to intervene in the wars between France and her enemies even though the United States was far more deeply "committed" to come to the aid of France by the terms of the Treaty of Alliance of 1778, than she was to intervene in Vietnam by the terms of the SEATO Treaty. Notwithstanding almost universal sympathy

* Henry David Thoreau, "On the Duty of Civil Disobedience," 1848.

for the peoples of Latin America who sought to throw off Spanish rule, we did not intervene militarily in that conflict. The ideas of "Manifest Destiny" and "Young America" dictated support to peoples everywhere struggling to throw off ancient tyrannies, but no President intervened militarily in the Greek struggle for independence from Turkey, the Italian uprisings against Austria, the Hungarian revolution of 1848 or other internal revolutions of that fateful year, Garibaldi's fight for Italian independence, the many Irish uprisings against Britain, in Ireland and even in Canada— close to home, that—or even mirabile dictu, the ten-year war of the Cubans against their Spanish overlords from 1868–78. Nor, in more modern times, did Presidents see fit to intervene on behalf of Jewish victims of pogroms, Turkish genocide against Armenians, Franco's overthrow of the Loyalist regime in Spain. Whether such abstention was always wise is a question we need not raise here. The point here is that in none of these situations did the Executive think it proper, or legal, to use his powers as Commander-in-Chief or as chief organ of foreign relations to commit the United States to military intervention in distant lands. With the sole exception of McKinley's unnecessary participation in the Boxer Expedition, that concept of executive powers belongs to the past quarter century. And if it should be asked why the United States should refrain from intervention in the internal struggles of other nations, even when her sympathies are deeply involved and her interests enlisted, it is perhaps sufficient to say that few of us would be prepared to endorse a principle that would have justified the intervention of Britain and France in the American Civil War— on behalf of the Confederacy of course—and that in international law you cannot really have it both ways.*

> COMMENT: Whether one agrees with Mr. Commager or not, it can-
> not be denied that he presents his case with coolheaded, balanced
> reason. What is more important, his argument is backed by indis-
> putable facts. It is worthwhile to note that one can make state-
> ments with facility and without thought; but when these statements
> are supported by historical facts, the listener or reader must stand
> up and pay attention. At any rate, Mr. Commager presents an im-
> pressive argument.

VI

Today scientist and Biblical scholar need not be at odds. In the 19th century scientists, having proved beyond doubt that certain details of the

*Henry Steele Commager, "The Misuse of Power," from The New Republic (April 17, 1971). Reprinted by Permission of The New Republic © 1971, Harrison-Blaine of New Jersey, Inc.

Bible could not be taken literally, seemed to be discrediting the Bible. For a while the Biblicist was in a dilemma: as a reasonable man, he could not deny scientific evidence; at the same time he was not prepared to deny the inspiration of God's book. Since that time, however, he has learned that certain parts of the Bible were never meant to be taken literally. In fact, scientific discoveries, far from disproving the Bible, provide a defense for it. Anthropology, for instance, has proved that the 1600 years allowed by the Bible for the period between Adam and the Deluge cannot be enough; there must have been at least 100,000. In the meantime archaeology has turned up thousands of clay tablets revealing the literature of Ancient Near Eastern contemporaries of Biblical writers. From such sources we learn that these people wrote in exactly the same way as the Hebrew authors. No one would think of taking these pagan authors literally, for they were not interested primarily in historical and scientific accuracy. And the same thing holds true for the Biblical authors. They, too, were often writing in a figurative, popular way. In the past, then, traditionalists and funda- mentalists were accustomed to taking everything in the Bible at face value and on only one level: i.e., an apple was an apple, a parted sea was a parted sea, a whale was a whale. Hence, when scientists showed them that everything could not be taken so, they were alarmed. They were frightened too easily, because these same scientists as well as literary critics also hold that the truth of a particular passage in the Bible or any work of literature is not impaired by the popular and figurative nature of the details but rather enhanced. Even as in *Hamlet,* so also in the Bible, to interpret symbolically and not just literally is to enrich, not impoverish, literature.

> COMMENT: *Through reasoning and factual recording we can show that the explanation of difficulties in Genesis is not a subterfuge. Scientific discoveries and higher criticism that at one time seemed to be destroying the accuracy of the Bible are now being used to defend it. This kind of reasoning is most effective in controversial subjects or in debating.*

VII

From evidence now available it is highly probable that the body of man did in fact evolve from the body of other, non-human animals. . . .

The question we must ask ourselves is: Can we reconcile this theory of evolution with the origin of man as presented in Genesis? The answer should be obvious. The Bible teaches that man was created by God. This fact alone does not contradict evolution because God is still the creator of man's body even though he creates it only mediately. The second account of creation seems, at first sight, to contradict the theory because it tells us that God molded man's body out of the dust of the ground. Note, however, that (1) this is clearly an anthropomorphism: God has no hands and does not work as a potter. (2) The author indicates by the context that he wishes to distinguish between man's body, which he has in common with other animals, and his soul, which comes directly from God. It is quite natural that he should say the body was made from clay because it returns to dust when death occurs, even as the bodies of all animals do. (3) Neglect of secondary causes (in this case, of intermediate animal forms) is common for the biblical writer. Actions are frequently attributed directly to their primary cause, God, even though we know that they were immediately produced by secondary causes. For example, even though it is certain that Job was born in a normal manner, he says: "Remember that thou hast made me of clay; and thou shalt turn me to dust again" (Job 10:9).

The Bible, therefore, merely affirms that God created man and that man's body comes from matter just as his immortal soul comes from God directly. The precise *manner* by which this action is described in Genesis is not to be taken in its strictly literal sense. In fine, the Bible does not exclude the possibility of natural evolution of man's body through a long series of less perfect animal forms.

COMMENT: *The theory of evolution is a bugaboo for some readers of the Bible. It needs plain and sensible explanation. Without getting technical this reconciliation of the Scriptures and science wraps up the whole question in short order. What is the effect of the enumeration in paragraph two? Although the passage is divided into three paragraphs, could it be logically only one paragraph? If so, what is the topic sentence?*

VIII

Is there any scientifically acceptable evidence that individual misconduct or social evils result from the reading of obscenity, hard-core or merely erotic or realistic? There are what I have styled elsewhere cigarette testimonials, by J. Edgar Hoover and others, which attest to the dire consequences of reading pornography. But there are no empirical studies by psychiatrists, psychologists, biologists, physiologists, criminologists, statisticians, sociologists or scientists generally, which would indicate such adverse effects on particular individuals or on society as a whole. Lacking such evidence, we cannot anticipate any calamitous results from a permissive attitude. If it should be established through objective testing at some later date that there is a measurable connection between delinquency, disease, crime, social evil, on the one hand, and obscenity on the other, it will be time enough to reject, or modify, an absolutist solution to the problem of dealing with the local people who thwart the Supreme Court.

It should be remembered, too, that there are undoubted ill consequences flowing from overeating, but we don't try to curb gluttony by law. We tried to create a temperate nation by law, but Prohibition was a disastrous failure, and we are still paying the price for it. We scarcely talk of banning cigarettes and smoking generally, despite the clearly established proof that disease and death are caused by tobacco. Why, then, should reading, the least baneful and, alas, least prevalent of human habits, be limited by law?

Those who are afraid that the filth will fall into the hands of children take that chance with liquor and tobacco. They ban the sale of such products to minors, and these laws are enforced often enough to be effective; the same should hold true for pornography. While the ostensible purpose of all censorship is to protect the young mind, there are very few instances of prosecution against those who actually sell to the young. Here, too, there will be difficulties as to definition, and doubt as to the evil effect of the reading matter. It is as an expedient rather than as a matter of principle that one makes this exception with respect to pre-adult readers.*

> COMMENT: This stand of Mr. Gertz is not beyond challenge. Yet consider what he has done and judge its effectiveness. We Americans have had our experience of Prohibition (ineffectual); we have evidence of the cancer threat of cigarettes (ads are now banned on TV but scarcely nowhere else); we have had admonitions about overeating (and we know, personally, the results). And we have our ban on pornography which no one seems to be able to define, and whose pernicious effects no one seems to be able to prove scientifically. All of these facts make for an inconvertible argument. But are there loopholes? Is it possible to present an argument for the opposite side? However, for the purpose of this book, it is most important for the student to recognize the use of inductive and deductive reasoning in the article of Mr. Gertz.

*Elmer Gertz, "An End to All Censorship," *The Nation* (July 5, 1965). Reprinted by permission of the publisher.

THE PARAGRAPH OF SPACE, TIME, NARRATION

Introduction

It is comparatively easy to write a paragraph of space, time, and narration, for in most cases all one needs to do is to follow the natural sequence of events or order of occurence. If one sets out to describe a cathedral, he begins from a distance seeing the cathedral from the outside and the facade as a whole. As he approaches, he notes details of the exterior that could not be seen at a distance. Next he enters the cathedral and describes his first impression of the semi-dark interior. As his vision clears, the structure and architecture are seen more accurately. He continues to give us details departing from the vestibule, continuing down the nave, and finally reaching the sanctuary. In other words, simply by following geographical and chronological lines in their proper sequence, the writer of this kind of paragraph will realize the enviable result: a work of order.

Above all, one must avoid distorting the point of view. If a cameraman is to catch an action, he cannot continually shift back and forth, from near to far, from top to bottom to center—except, perhaps, for comic effects or, as in an art film, for an intentional and appropriate reaction. Ordinarily if one is describing a face, he cannot go from forehead, to mouth, to hair, to nose to eyebrows. A line of direction must be established and carefully maintained. Occasionally, however, and for dramatic effects, one can start at a point other than the beginning. He can, for instance, plunge in medias res: "Susan wondered how she could have gotten herself into such a mess. There she was at midnight in a strange town, alone, frightened, half starved. She began to recall the day's events. At six o'clock Tom had called. After dinner, they had started out for the drive-in when . . . ." Occasionally, too, one can start at the very end, retreat, and then proceed with the beginning. Thus, one could open with the funeral of a renowned, public figure. Thousands are standing in the rain, mourning his departure. His wife, dressed in appropriate black, seems to be the saddest of them all. A great statesman has departed. After the funeral a reporter interviews the widow only to find out that she is not mourning her husband's departure at all. Slowly she begins to unfold the history of his career, revealing for the first time that the "great statesman" was nothing but a cad, a philanderer, an unfaithful husband, a dishonest, conniving politician.

A preference of active over passive voice and an accent on precision are necessary for all kinds of paragraphs, but they are especially important in this kind. Be as accurate and direct as possible about just what happened, just when, just where. The rest should follow with ease.

I

The *people* came out of their houses and smelled the hot stinging air and covered their noses from it. *And* the children came out of the houses, but they did not run or shout as they would have done after a rain. *Men* stood by their fences and looked at the ruined corn, drying fast now, only a little green showing through the film of dust. The *men* were silent they did not move often. And the *women* came out of the houses to stand beside their men—to feel whether this time the men would break. The *women* studied the men's faces secretly, for the corn could go, as long as something else remained. The *children* stood near by, *drawing figures in the dust* with bare toes, and the children sent exploring sense out to see whether men and women would break. The *children* peeked at the faces of the men and women, and then drew careful lines *in the dust with their toes*. *Horses* came to the watering trough and nuzzled the water to clear the surface dust. *After a while* the faces of the watching men lost their bemused perplexity and became hard and angry and resistant. *Then* the women knew they were safe and that there was no break. Then they asked, what'll we do? And the men replied, I don't know. *But* it was all right. The *women* knew it was all right, and the watching *children* knew it was all right. *Women and children* knew deep in themselves that no misfortune was too great to bear if their

generic, includes all: men, women, children
transitional—often repeated in paragraph

active voice throughout

six sentences: two for men, two for women, two for children

women's position between men and children

note repetitions here and elsewhere—antiphonal effect

presents nonthinking element in picture

note indicated time sequence

transitional

mentioned separately, then together, then separately

men were whole. The *women* went into the houses to their work, and the *children* began to play, but cautiously at first. As the day went forward the sun became less red. It flared down on the dust-blanketed land. The *men* sat in the doorways of their houses; their hands were busy with sticks and little rocks. The men sat still—thinking—figuring.*

pivotal change from human beings, to the inanimate, back to human beings

paragraph ends with men as most important group

II

Jamaica is one of the most foreign of Caribbean countries. Its Americanized hostelries for Bermuda-shorted tourists and their air-conditioned wives are but loosely painted onto the jagged, gaping Jamaican culture. But the Jamaica Tourist Board is highly effective, and the placid tourists are led around by their pudgy, green wallets, so dazzled by the physical beauty that they rarely see anything of the real Jamaica, one of the most invigorating and beautiful of all the islands. If Jamaica presents perplexing questions to the inquisitive young traveler, the answers are well-worth seeking.

You'll fly into Montego Bay, because, even if you come in from Miami, capital of false hopes and tinsel gods, you will not be prepared for the cultural shock of Kingston. You must travel by car. This is vital if you want to escape the ludicrous runaround of the typical Jamaican tourist grind. If there are only one or two of you, and your funds are really low, you'll want to hitchhike. It's generally accepted here; just stand at the side of the road and point cheerfully at everyone going your way (Jamaicans are especially fond of beards). Avoid it at night, however, unless you have a secret death wish. Jamaican drivers are the worst in the western hemisphere.**

COMMENT: *Information is most important. What do you think of the two adjectives, "Americanized" and "Bermuda-shorted"? Are they effective or not? It is not so much knowledge of the Caribbean countries that matters as the ability to communicate that knowledge. Try to communicate your knowledge of your home town (city) to someone unfamiliar with your environment.*

III

R. J. Bowman, who for fourteen years had traveled for a shoe company through Mississippi, drove his Ford along a rutted dirt path. It was a long day! The time did not seem to clear the noon hurdle and settle into soft afternoon. The sun, keeping its strength here even in winter, stayed at the top of the sky, and every time Bowman stuck his head out of the dusty car to stare up the road, it seemed to reach a long arm down and push the top of his head, right through his hat—like the practical joke of an old drummer, long on the road. It made him feel all the more angry and helpless. He was feverish, and he was not quite sure of the way.

This was his first day back on the road after a long siege of influenza. He had had very high fever, and dreams, and had become weakened and pale, enough to tell the difference in the mirror, and he could not think clearly. . . . All afternoon, in the midst of his anger, and for no reason, he had thought of his dead grandmother. She had been a comfortable soul. Once more Bowman wished he could fall into the big feather bed that had been in her room. . . . Then he forgot her again.*

COMMENT: *Miss Welty gives us, as usual, a fine beginning for her short story. It sets us immediately into the action—in time and space. While doing this, she also manages to give us an intimation of what R. J. Bowman is like.*

IV

When I reached C Company lines, which were at the top of the hill, I paused and looked back at the camp, just coming into full view below me through the grey mist of early morning. We were leaving that day. When we marched in, three months before, the place was under snow; now the first leaves of spring were unfolding. I had reflected then that, whatever scenes of desolation lay ahead of us, I never feared one more brutal than this, and I reflected now that it had no single happy memory for me.

Here love had died between me and the army.

Here the train lines ended, so that men returning fuddled from Glasgow could doze in their seats until roused by the conductress at their journey's end. There was some way to go from the tram-stop to the camp gates; a quarter of a mile in which they could button their blouses and straighten their caps before passing the guardroom, a quarter of a mile in which concrete gave place to grass at the road's edge. This was the extreme limit

*Eudora Welty, "Death of a Traveling Salesman," from *A Curtain of Green and Other Stories.* Reprinted by permission of Harcourt Brace Jovanovich, Inc.

of the city, a fringe of drift-wood above high-water mark. Here the close, homogeneous territory of housing estates and cinemas ended and the hinterland began.

The camp stood where, until quite lately, had been pasture and ploughland; the farmhouse still stood in a fold of the hill and had served us for battalion offices; ivy still supported part of what had once been the walls of a fruit garden; half an acre of mutilated old trees behind the wash-houses survived of an orchard. The place had been marked for destruction before the army came to it. Had there been another year of peace, there would have been no farmhouse, no wall, no apple trees. Already half a mile of concrete road lay between bare clay banks, and on either side a chequer of open ditches showed where the municipal contractors had designed a system of drainage. Another year of peace would have made the place part of the neighbouring suburb. Now the huts where we had wintered waited their turn for destruction.*

> COMMENT: This is a good example of the then-and-now technique. What is the effect of the one-sentence second paragraph? Is Evelyn Waugh consistent in his use of past and past-perfect tense? Notice the first verbs in sentences 2 and 3.

V

One step brought us into the family sitting-room, without any introductory lobby or passage: they call it here "the house" pre-eminently. It includes kitchen and parlour, generally; but I believe at Wuthering Heights the kitchen is forced to retreat altogether into another quarter: at least I distinguished a chatter of tongues, and a clatter of culinary utensils, deep within; and I observed no signs of roasting, boiling, or baking, about the huge fire-place; nor any glitter of copper saucepans and tin cullenders on the walls. One end, indeed, reflected splendidly both light and heat from ranks of immense pewter dishes, interspersed with silver jugs and tankards, towering row after row, on a vast oak dresser, to the very roof. The latter had never been underdrawn: its entire anatomy lay bare to an inquiring eye, except where a frame of wood laden with oatcakes and clusters of legs of beef, mutton, and ham, concealed it. Above the chimney were sundry villainous old guns, and a couple of horse-pistols: and, by way of ornament, three gaudily-painted canisters disposed along its ledge. The floor was of smooth white stone; the chairs, high-backed, primitive structures, painted green: one or two heavy black ones lurking in the shade. In an arch under

---

* Evelyn Waugh, Prologue to *Brideshead Revisited* (Boston: Little, Brown and Company, 1945).

the dresser, reposed a huge, liver-coloured bitch pointer, surrounded by a swarm of squealing puppies; and other dogs haunted other recesses.*

> COMMENT: It is interesting to note the order of Miss Bronte's observations. She has just entered the sitting room. The kitchen, usually a part of this room, is in another quarter of the house. She can surmise this fact positively by her hearing, and negatively by her not seeing any kitchen utensils. The fire-place is the center of her description. She describes what is around, above it, and beneath it.

VI

Once a day a cheap, gaudy packet arrived upward from St. Louis, and another downward from Keokuk. Before these events, the day was glorious with expectancy; after them, the day was a dead and empty thing. Not only the boys, but the whole village, felt this. After all these years I can picture that old time to myself now, just as it was then: the white town drowsing in the sunshine of a summer's morning; the streets empty, or pretty nearly so; one or two clerks sitting in front of the Water Street stores, with their splint-bottomed chairs tilted back against the walls, chins on breasts, hats slouched over their faces, asleep—with shingle-shavings enough around to show what broke them down; a sow and a litter of pigs loafing along the sidewalk, doing a good business in watermelon rinds and seeds; two or three lonely little freight piles scattered about the "levee"; a pile of "skids" on the slope of the stone-paved wharf, and the fragrant town drunkard asleep in the shadow of them; two or three wood flats at the head of the wharf, but nobody to listen to the peaceful lapping of the wavelets against them; the great Mississippi, the majestic, the magnificent Mississippi, rolling its mile-wide tide along, shining in the sun; the dense forest away on the other side; the "point" above the town, and the "point" below, bounding the river-glimpse and turning it into a sort of sea, and withal a very still and brilliant and lonely one. Presently a film of dark smoke appears above one of those remote "points"; instantly a negro drayman, famous for his quick eye and prodigious voice, lifts up the cry, "S-t-e-a-m-boat a-comin'!" and the scene changes! The Town drunkard stirs, the clerks wake up, a furious clatter of drays follows, every house and store pours out a human contribution, and all in a twinkling the dead town is alive and moving. Drays, carts, men, boys, all go hurrying from many quarters to a common center, the wharf. Assembled there, the people fasten their eyes upon the coming boat as upon a wonder they are seeing

* Emily Bronte, *Wuthering Heights.*

for the first time. And the boat *is* rather a handsome sight, too. She is long and sharp and trim and pretty; she has two tall, fancy-topped chimneys, with a gilded device of some kind swung between them; a fanciful pilot-house, all glass and "gingerbread," perched on top of the "texas" deck behind them; the paddle-boxes are gorgeous with a picture or with gilded rays above the boat's name; the boiler-deck, the hurricane-deck, and the texas deck are fenced and ornamented with clean white railings; there is a flag gallantly flying from the jack-staff; the furnace doors are open and the fires glaring bravely; the upper decks are black with passengers; the captain stands by the big bell, calm, imposing, the envy of all; great volumes of the blackest smoke are rolling and tumbling out of the chimneys—a husbanded grandeur created with a bit of pitch pine just before arriving at a town; the crew are grouped on the forecastle; the broad stage is run far out over the port bow, and an envied deckhand stands picturesquely on the end of it with a coil of rope in his hand; the pent steam is screaming through the gauge-cocks; the captain lifts his hand, a bell rings, the wheels stop; then they turn back, churning the water to foam, and the steamer is at rest. Then such a scramble as there is to get aboard, and to get ashore, and to take in freight and to discharge freight, all at one and the same time; and such a yelling and cursing as the mates facilitate it all with! Ten minutes later the steamer is under way again, with no flag on the jack-staff and no black smoke issuing from the chimneys. After ten more minutes the town is dead again, and the town drunkard asleep by the skids once more.*

> COMMENT: *There are three stages in this description: before, during, and after. Do these three stages allow for three paragraphs, in accordance with our style today? Which of the three stages is the longest? Why? Which is the shortest and why? Is there any significance in the fact that the description ends with a reference to the town drunk? This paragraph is an excellent example of narration blended with description.*

*Mark Twain, "Steamboat A-comin'," *Life on the Mississippi* (1875).

THE OPENING AND CONCLUDING PARAGRAPH

Introduction

Out of context, how can one determine what is an effective, appropriate opening or closing paragraph. Impossible. Neither paragraph is an isolated unit and without reference to or a knowledge of the entire essay we remain unable to judge. The advice given and the examples offered in this *Handbook* limp, and that is an understatement. Our only hope is that they will offer trivial (but not wasteful) help for the novice.

ADVICE ON OPENING PARAGRAPHS

1. Often the best way to begin a short paper is not to bother with an introduction at all. Start right in. After you have finished your paper, you may find one of two solutions: a) the opening paragraph that escaped you at the start may come with no pain or exertion after the body of the paper is completed. In this connection, it is good to remember that an introduction to a rather long paper or a book is *always* written after all the rest is finished. After all, as in the case with people, one cannot introduce what one does not know. b) Your paper may be of such a nature that you do not need a specially developed opening paragraph.

2. Do not waste your own or your reader's time by opening with superfluous trifles. To open your paper by saying that now you are taking up your pen and finding paper and adjusting your lamp in order to write is to open with unmitigated twaddle.

3. It follows then that one should begin with something arresting, dramatic, important. Before one can sustain interest he must first catch it. Ignore the "arresting" and "important" if you wish, but do make the opening important—if it is important, it is also interesting, and perhaps arresting.

4. For a less formal paper a casual approach that allows your personality to show is often desirable. Look at Malcolm Muggeridge, Dwight MacDonald, James Reston, D. H. Lawrence, James Joyce, Eudora Welty, John Updike, and a thousand other good writers. What catches your attention from the very beginning? Style. Personality. Good writing is like good looks. What catches your attention when you see two girls who are almost equally graced by nature? Not looks, not clothes, not makeup; but style, personality.

5. Keep in mind the kind of mood or impression or effect you are striving to create. Also, as always, keep in mind for whom you are writing.

6. Never begin with an apology for your ineptitude or a humble negation of the paper's value. If the paper is inferior, the instructor will soon find that out for himself. He does not need a prompter. Besides, if you believe the paper is poor, then you should not hand it in.

7. Length of introduction should bear some correspondence to the length of the whole. A long paper may sometimes need only a short introduction; a short paper of, let us say, five hundred words cannot bear an introduction of three hundred.

ADVICE ON CLOSING PARAGRAPHS

1. End with a strong or main point.

2. Bring your paper full circle by, indirectly at least, referring back to the opening.

3. An effective summary is at times a good device.

4. Do not end your paper with the inane, the irrelevant, the needlessly repetitious.

5. Do not end with an apology for mistakes or an explanation of why the paper is not better than it is ("I attended the prom last night; I had a headache last week; I had an examination in mathematics yesterday").

6. Do not say more than you need to. If you have said everything that you think is necessary and cannot think of anything more to add, then in all likelihood you already have your conclusion.

7. Above all, do not end with a pious exhortation or overt bit of moralizing. You are to write narrative and expository papers, not sermons.

Opening Paragraphs

I

You would recognize him even in a crowd. The sculptured, bronzed, profile of one of those Roman emperors about whom he writes so brilliantly; the massive grace of a soldier and mountaineer who, at the age of sixty-five, moves nimbly down rockpaths of his island to plunge into the dawn cold of the Mediterranean; the bearing of a man who has sired eight children and seventy books; who has lived by his pen and his wits in tenacious integrity and who, after years in comparative neglect, is beginning to loom over the horizon as the finest and most prolific man of letters now writing in English. His name is Robert Graves.*

* George Steiner, from "The Genius of Robert Graves," *The Kenyon Review*, XXII (summer, 1960), 340.

COMMENT:　*This is an immediate, direct opening. There is no pre-liminary posturing, no time lost in getting started. Note the dra-matic punch of the last sentence. Would it have been more effec-tive to name Robert Graves in the first sentence? Explain.*

II

The only possible excuse for this book is that it is an answer to a challenge. Even a bad shot is dignified when he accepts a duel. When some time ago I published a series of hasty but sincere papers, under the name of "Heretics," several critics for whose intellect I have a warm respect (I may mention specially Mr. G. S. Street) said it was all very well for me to tell everybody to affirm his cosmic theory, but that I had carefully avoided supporting my precepts with example. "I will begin to worry about my philosophy," said Mr. Street, "when Mr. Chesterton has given us his." It was perhaps an incautious suggestion to make to a person only too ready to write books upon the feeblest provocation. But after all, though Mr. Street has inspired and created this book, he need not read it. If he does read it, he will find that in its pages I have attempted in a vague and personal way, in a set of mental pictures rather than in a series of deduc-tions, to state the philosophy in which I have come to believe. I will not call it my philosophy; for I did not make it. God and humanity made it; and it made me.*

COMMENT:　*This is an informal, leisurely opening that suits well Chesterton's purpose here. He first tries to sell himself before sell-ing his beliefs.*

III

Several weeks ago I received a newspaper clipping from a friend at the University of Wisconsin reporting the death of Miss Ruth Wallerstein in England, the victim of an automobile accident. Somehow I had never seriously thought of death and Miss Wallerstein; for when I knew her she was already a legend, remarkable, beautiful, and imperishable. I remember the many times I had seen her drive her car over the confusing, angling streets of Madison, and with what awe I had witnessed her impetuous and oftentimes illegal turns into one-way streets and no-exit courts. Miss Wallerstein, I knew, was above the machinery that carried her, for she lived in a finer world than ours.

*G. K. Chesterton, from *Orthodoxy*. Reprinted by permission of Dodd, Mead & Co. and The Bodley Head, Ltd. Copyright 1908, 1935 by G. K. Chesterton.

When I first enrolled in a course under her, I was not disposed to like Miss Wallerstein. I had heard graduate students speak with reverence of her scholarship, her insights, and her appreciation of what was "central" to the humanistic tradition in western life, a subject that seemed so generally known that any brilliancy a scholar might bring to it seemed wasted to me. I had heard of her great personal beauty, but beauty to me meant Garbo or Dietrich, so I was not at all prepared for what I saw that first day: a woman of average size wearing a pince-nex over kindly but rather misty eyes, her remarkable gray hair topped by an unusual hat, all feathers and bows. As soon as she began to call the roll I knew that, although I might never understand a word she spoke, I could not drop the course. For Miss Wallerstein possessed the most beautiful voice I have ever heard. I listened to her read from Hamlet many times—the "If ever thou didst hold me in thy heart" passage was her favorite—and I have listened to Gielgud and Evans and Olivier and Neville read it too, but none with the power and magic of Miss Wallerstein. And whenever I see Hamlet on the stage, I see Miss Wallerstein in Hamlet's place, and the black tights are becoming to her too. Once a witty female graduate said in my presence, "Look at the figure wasted on that old—scholar!"*

> COMMENT: By use of narration Mr. DeVitis is able to give us the occasion and background for his article. He rapidly adds details, incident, and even a quotation to paint a fond portrait of a remarkable woman.

IV

This year was 1914. A wiry young doctor returned to Massachusetts General Hospital after a year in London. Grinning proudly, he pointed to a strange machine he had brought back with him. It was, he explained to his fellow Boston physicians, an electrical device to record the beat of the human heart. With its help, he told them, he was going to concentrate his talents on the little-known diseases of the heart.

Some of his friends and teachers were alarmed. So little was known about that vital organ, they warned, that such a specialization would be one of the least fruitful in medicine. If he did what he intended, he would be side-tracked into so narrow a field that his voice would never again be heard.

Forty-one years later, on September 25, 1955, the entire world listened to what Paul Dudley White, then 69, had to say . . . .**

*A. A. DeVitis, from "For Rememberance." Reprinted from College English, May 1960, copyright 1969 by the National Council of Teachers of English. Reprinted by permission of the publisher.
**Theodore Berland, "Paul Dudley White," from Today's Health, published by The American Medical Association.

opening paragraphs

V

Any number of people have defended Milton's Satan, from their different points of view, but I believe I am actually original in defending his Delilah; and yet her case is much the easier to defend; it is a pushover. Milton himself only cared to handle difficult cases, just like Perry Mason and similar good characters, and was busy at the time on the case of Samson; but he needed a real Delilah for his play, and the lady he produced would be given heavy damages, by any British or American jury, as a deeply wronged wife. I did not examine her case because I was hungry for even greater absurdity than defending Satan, but from wanting to be consistent; and the results, though you may feel they make the case for Satan less important, also make it more understandable. We must respect Milton's firm sense of justice towards his characters. It has been thought that he was "unconsciously" in favor of his Satan; but you would probably need to get a fair way down in his Unconsciousness before you got underneath his dislike for Delilah.*

COMMENT: *History plays an important part in introducing this article. Although the paper is a formal one, allusions to Perry Mason and "a deeply wronged wife" help to set a graceful, timely air.*

VI

I live in a fantastic world, a fabulous land, a city of my imagination. There wondrous things befall people, and I have had my share of these adventures. I shall tell you something about them, profiting by the fact that on New Year's Eve people are inclined to listen to all sorts of fantasies.**

COMMENT: *Nothing could be more direct and appropriate than "I shall tell you something about them . . . ."*

VII

A major campaign speech of a presidential candidate may take but thirty minutes to deliver, but it may represent the end product of fifty staff

---

*William Empson, from *Milton's God.* Copyright 1961 by William Empson. Reprinted by permission of New Directions Publishing Corporation and Chatto & Windus Ltd.
**Vladimir Dudintsev, from "A New Year's Fable," translated from the Russian by George Reavey. From the *Partisan Review* (Spring 1960). © 1960 by the Partisan Review. Reprinted by permission of the publisher and the author.

members devoted to research, planning, and writing. In this paper a study is made of the organization, purpose, and function of Adlai Stevenson's 1956 speech staff. What pre-1956 campaign planning was carried on? What research was done prior to the writing of the campaign speeches? How did Stevenson select his speech staff and whom did he select? How was the speech occasion planned? How were the campaign speeches prepared?*

> COMMENT: *This opens with a statement of purpose (second sentence). Note that by asking these questions, he commits himself to their answers.*

VIII

We had been planning the trip for over a year. Pinching, scraping and going without sodas, we had salvaged from our allowances and the small-time jobs we each had found the preceding vacation the sum of $80.00, which was the cost of a minimum passage on a Canadian Pacific liner of the cabin class. Our respective families had augmented our finances by letters of credit generous enough to permit us to live for three months abroad if not in the lap of luxury, at least on the knees of comfort. For months we had been exchanging letters brimming over with rapturous plans and lyric anticipation and now June had really rolled around and the happy expectancy of the brides-to-be of that year had nothing on us.**

IX

I can show you what is left. After the pride, passion, agony, and bemused aspiration, what is left is in our hands. Here are the scraps of newspaper, more than a century old, splotched and yellowed and huddled together in a library, like November leaves abandoned by the wind, damp, and bleached out, back to the stables or in a fence corner of a vacant lot. Here are the diaries, the documents, and the letters, yellow too, bound in neat bundles with tape so stiffened and tired that it parts almost unresisting at your touch. Here are the records of what happened in that courtroom, all the words taken down. Here is the manuscript he himself wrote, day

---

*Russel Windes, Jr., "Adlai E. Stevenson's Speech Staff in the 1956 Campaign," from *Quarterly Journal of Speech*, XLVI, February 1960. Reprinted by permission of Russel Windes.
**Cornelia Otis Skinner and Emily Kimbrough, from *Our Hearts Were Young and Gay*. Reprinted by permission of Dodd, Mead & Co., Inc., and Constable & Co. Ltd. Copyright 1942 by Dodd, Mead & Co., Inc.

after day, as he waited in his cell, telling his story. The letters of his script lean forward in their haste. Haste toward what? The bold stroke of the quill catches on the rough paper, fails, resumes, moves on in its race against time, to leave time behind, or in its rush to meet time at last the devoted and appointed place. To whom was he writing, rising from his mire or leaning from his flame to tell his story? The answer is easy. He was writing to us.*

Closing Paragraphs

I

In the event of total confusion, it may be useful to remember Samuel Johnson's dictum: "Dictionaries are like watches: the worst is better than none, and the best cannot be expected to go quite true."**

COMMENT: *A conclusion with an apt quotation.*

II

Whatever else may be said about Hitler, his death was in character. The operatic finale in the bunker below a flaming, shattered Berlin epitomizes the tawdry, melodramatic Hitlerian *Geist,* the solemn, futile personal testament, distributing state offices in a disintegrated government among the surviving faithful; the ghastly nuptials with Eva Braun; the murder-suicide of Hitler and his spouse and the Goebbelses with their six children, all of whom were poisoned; the cremation of the corpses with aviation gasoline in the Reich Chancellery above the bunker, amid the shelling on oncoming Russian artillery.

Perhaps deliberately, Hitler even contrived to touch his fate with mystery, for he ordered that his corpse be burned until nothing remained. It is virtually certain that he died in the bunker, but no one has produced visible proof. In the unlikely event that Adolph Hitler should one day emerge from the wastes of Siberia, Patagonia or the Sahara, what, if anything, would be done with the living relic of the terrible era that he so largely shaped? †

*Robert Penn Warren, from *World Enough and Time,* copyright 1950 by Random House, Inc. Reprinted by permission of the publisher.
**Felicia Lamport, from "Dictionaries, Our Language Right or Wrong," *Harper's Magazine* (September 1959). Reprinted by permission of Harper & Row, Publishers.
† Telford Taylor, from "Hitler: A Portrait in Retrospect." *The New York Times Magazine,* April 19, 1959. ⓒ 1959 by The New York Times Company. Reprinted by permission.

III

It was almost impossible to believe that all about us the countryside was swarming with columns of troops—German, Serbian, Russian and Cossack—headed toward Belgrade, some to defend it, others to attack it, in a battle that was to take the lives of thousands in only a few days time. Here in Baljevo all was peace and calm. No staff cars, sirens blazing, sped through the streets. No colonels with bulging briefcases hurried from conference to conference. No motorcycle messengers broke the quiet with the unmuffled roar of their engines. Here where the front was only a few miles away, in any direction you chose, no one thought about "divisional slices" and P.O.L. and PX's and Motor Pools. It was almost a relief that a solid line of enemy troops along the Dalmatian Coast and south across Macedonia separated us from the Frankenstein armies of the West with their colossal staffs and hordes of camp-following, overworked pay clerks and code clerks and officious stenographers and M.P.'s London seemed another world—which I didn't want to see again until the war was over and it had demobilized itself for good.*

> COMMENT: As he prepares to leave the scene, Mr. Thayer takes a final look around. This is much similar to a movie fadeout that leaves a dramatic picture in the viewer's mind.

IV

On the grounds as relative as these, there has been and will be a spate of other Hamlets. For Hamlet and Shakespeare's other great characters are so rich in possible meanings because they are fashioned on the essentially human principle of both/and rather than either/or. Hamlet is more than the sum of his paradoxes; he is the paradox of man seen whole. All one knows for certain is that being Hamlet is Hamlet's tragedy—as being himself is everyman's.

Paraphrasing Keats, it might be said that Shakespeare's plays lead a life of allegory, and human existence is the commentary upon them. Every age and every man, in his seven ages, finds a reflection in Shakespeare's universal mirror. The passion and the poetry echo in the corridors of the mind, and truer than "the infancy of truth" will go on echoing to the last of time.**

*Charles W. Thayer, from "In the Woods with Tito" in Bears in the Caviar. Reprinted by permission of Brandt & Brandt.
**Time Magazine, July 4, 1960, from "To Man From Mankind's Heart." Reprinted by permission from Time. The Weekly Newsmagazine; Copyright Time, Inc. 1960.

closing paragraphs

COMMENT: Time ends its study of Shakespeare by reaching a peak. This is not so much a summary as a conclusive and consummating statement.

V

As in France and Italy, television in England operates for no more than seven or eight hours a day. This means that the ever-present threat of running out of material can just about be held off from one week to the next. A great many viewing hours are given to old Hollywood movies, or wasted on material that ought to be given to sound radio; but this is a world-wide condition. One day, if reason prevails, radio and TV will agree to share the available resources, in which case there will be plenty for both. With a combined TV and radio program we should be able to hear the news without having to waste our eyesight on the newsreader's appearance, listen to music without wondering whether the tympanist is going to fall off the stand, and generally give back some self-respect to our organs of hearing. When anything of a visual nature crops up, the screen could take over. But before any such sensible arrangement becomes possible, the popular mind will have to abandon Darwinism, or its own version of Darwinism, and thus get rid of the notion that each successive invention must swallow the one before and take over all its duties.*

COMMENT: The conclusion combines two important aspects of this kind of survey: it provides a summary of the condition at present; it speculates on what the situation in the future might be.

VI

To sum up, then, I would say that as of now Catholic literature in this country is just past its embryonic state. There are indications that a period of tremendous growth and development is in the offing and not too distant. In many cases, the clues to substantiate this belief are often intangible but when correctly interpreted lead to one conclusion—at least to one interested observer—that we are about to enter a period of unprecedented and exciting developments in the Catholic literary field.**

*John Wain, from "Is TV Livelier Abroad?" Reprinted with permission from *Holiday,* © 1959 The Curtis Publishing Co.
**John J. Delaney, from "Report on a Literary Contest." Reprinted from *The Critic,* XVIII, June–July 1960.

VII

Perhaps it was inevitable that Dickens should fail to understand America, that he should write about the new sprawling republic from a point of view which narrowed and distorted much of what he saw. And yet, his increasingly hostile and somber conception of the United States did not prevent him from realizing that he was confronted with an artistic problem which transcended *Chuzzlewit* and his views of America: the problem of how to take emotionally charged autobiography and mold it into art. In subsequent novels, in *David Copperfield* and *Great Expectations,* for example, he solved his crucial problem. But those later solutions had as their prototype the painful testing ground of *Chuzzlewit.* For the frustrations and difficulties which Dickens struggled with when he attempted to transmute his American experiences into fiction eventually enabled him to push forward in later novels to a richer and more mature art *

VIII

We suggest therefore that there are significant twists and inversions in the characters and themes of Greene's novels and plays and that these twists and inversions pivot around the same radical conflicts regarding the problem and the mystery of sin.

Briefly, there are four points we would like to suggest for further discussion of Greene's mastery of conflict:

First: Greene uses frequently the paradoxical principle that God appears to be psychologically most present when theologically He is most remote.

Second: Just as a person in the state of grace has within his soul the beginnings of eternal life and should therefore be supernaturally happy, so the sinner in the state of theological separation from God is experiencing, in his psychological-moral condition of guilt and sin, some of the terrifying reality of the pain of loss.

Third: There is a compatibility between theological faith and rational disbelief (in the sense of dissatisfaction with rational arguments) but it cannot be pushed too far. Possibly Greene does push the principle too far on occasion.

Fourth: There are significant twists in the themes and characterizations of Greene which center around the fundamental conflicts involved in the problem and mystery of sin.**

* Harry Stone, from "Dickens' Use of His American Experiences in *Martin Chuzzlewit.*" Reprinted from PMLA, LXXII, June 1957 by permission.
**Thomas A. Wassmer, S. J., from "Graham Green: A Look At His Sinners." Reprinted from *The Critic,* XVIII, January 1960.

closing paragraphs

IX

I took her hand in mine, and we went out of the ruined place; and as the morning mists had risen long ago when I first left the forge, so the evening mists were rising now, and in all the broad expanse of tranquil light they showed to me, I saw no shadow of another parting from her.*

COMMENT: This is the celebrated, and to some compromising, last paragraph of Dickens' Great Expectations. Whatever its demerits the original ending was far less optimistic—it has four merits: 1) it lends a lyrical charm to a novel that is in essence a love story; 2) it takes the reader back to the very beginning of the story, to the forge, to the rising mists; 3) it was morning then, it is evening now; 4) it strikes a note of nostalgia and hope, with no complacent, simple solution.

*Charles Dickens, Great Expectations (1861).

INDEX

CORRECTION SYMBOLS

Grammar and Usage

see pages

Agr	error in AGREEMENT: pronoun-antecedent or subject-verb	76–79; 60; 10–12
CS	COMMA SPLICE error	29–31
Dng	DANGLING MODIFIER; modification error	57–58
Emp	lack of EMPHASIS in the sentence	69–71
Frag	sentence FRAGMENT; incomplete sentence	9–10
Gr	error in GRAMMAR	3–17; 80–82
K	AWKWARD sentence; recast for emphasis	69–71
MM	MISPLACED MODIFIER; modification error	55–57; 14–15
‖	faulty PARALLELISM; unbalanced sentence structure	60–63; 34–37; 20–21
Ref	faulty or indefinite REFERENCE of pronouns	76–79
S	error in SENTENCE STRUCTURE	8–17; 65–66
Sq M	SQUINTING MODIFIER; modification error	57
Sub	faulty or inadequate SUBORDINATION of dependent ideas	65–66; 73; 29–31
T	wrong TENSE of verb	81; 60–62
WW	WRONG WORD or wrong verb	80–81; 84–89

Words

Clq	inappropriate COLLOQUIAL expression	84
D	faulty DICTION; check the glossary	84–89
Sp	SPELLING error; correct	
W	WORDINESS; compress the sentence	69–71